D0884319

GUY DAVENPORT

Thasos and Ohio
Poems and Translations 1950-1980

NORTH POINT PRESS
San Francisco
1986

Printed in the United States of America
Published in England by Carcanet Press Ltd.
Library of Congress Catalogue Card Number:85-72989
ISBN:0-86547-227-0

FOR CHRISTOPHER MIDDLETON

Where stone lies the body also
Borne under sun and circumstance
Would navigate through the undertow
Whether of seawave or breathed utterance

ACKNOWLEDGEMENTS

"The Resurrection in Cookham Churchyard" was published in *Poetry* August 1967, and as a book in 1982, by Jordan Davies, New York. The translations of Archilochos, Sappho, and Alkman, earlier versions of which came out variously in *Arion*, *Poetry*, and *The Hudson Review*, are from *Archilochos Sappho Alkman*, University of California Press, 1980 and 1984. "Poem: For Lu Chi's *Wen Fu* (302 A.D.)" was published in *The Hudson Review*, "At Marathon" in *Parnassus*, and "The Medusa" in Edward Field's anthology, *A Geography of Poets*, Bantam Books, New York 1979 and as a pamphlet by David Orr and Gray Zeitz, Louisville, Kentucky, 1984. "Poem Begun by Ronald Johnson", "Swan" (which figures, distributed through the text, in my "Christ Preaching at the Henley Regatta", *Da Vinci's Bicycle*, The John Hopkins University Press, 1979), "Swans", published in *The Kentucky Review*, and "Beyond Punt and Cush", published in *The Hollow Spring Review*, were all reprinted as a book, *Goldfinch Thistle Star*, by Red Ozier Press, New York, 1983. The translations of the first and a fragment of the fifth *Duino Elegies* figure in *Apples and Pears*, North Point Press, Berkeley, 1984. "Ohio", from the same text, is an extension of a Shaker song. "For Lorine Niedecker" was published in *Epitaphs for Lorine*, edited by Jonathan Williams, The Jargon Society, North Carolina, 1973. "For Cousin Jonathan" appeared in *Truck*, and "For Basil Bunting" in *Madeira & Toasts for Basil Bunting's 75th Birthday*, The Jargon Society, 1977. The translations from Anakreon were published in *Conjunctions*. "Springtime and Autumn", "Amphora and Daughterleaf" and "Fire, October, Eyes" are excerpts from *Flowers and Leaves*, The Jargon Society, 1966. "1880" was published in *Conjunctions*; it is a translation from the Hebrew in that its author, Harold Schimmel, the distinguished Israeli poet, provided me with a trot and vetted the translation. The translations of Diogenes and Herondas are from *Herakleitos and Diogenes* and *The Mimes of Herondas*, both by Grey Fox Press, San Francisco, 1979 and 1981 respectively.

Contents

Thasos and Ohio

The Resurrection in Cookham Churchyard

The Cookham dead began to rise
When God with April in his eyes
Ended in O its midst the night.
To dogwood flowered hard and white,
To rain and violets overhead,
Sharp music lifted up the dead,
In cuckoo song and silence born,
A silver brilliant hunting horn.
Through opened grass Sir Jonas Moore
Swims upward to the chapel door.
Broken earth in her ancient hands,
Here Sarah Tubb the prophet stands.
In pleated light and diamond bone
Comes Petronella Elphinstone.
Sir Edward Coke in rotten lace
Sits up with wonder on his face.
Michael Ventris surfaces near
The round and pious Edward Lear.
Thoda Pigbone with the stick-pin
Finery she was buried in,
All cackle, warts, and raddled gums,
From troubled earth triumphant comes.
Karl Marx so white, so rich of beard,
By Richard Porson stands upreared.
The drummers of Tobruk climb out,
The buglers at the Dunkirk rout.
Leander Hosmer, dressed in red
Among the Macedonian dead,
Bassoon, the Regimental Band,
The angel's resurrecting hand,
Fire, grace, and water in a wave,
Accepts and rises from his grave.
Bright wakened eyes to starlight turn
And tongues in flaming splendor burn,
Till spirit sheer in breath and light
Stands naked to his naked sight,

The miller, husbandman, and wheat,
God, God the eater and to eat,
The thresher who with stormy hand
Shall winnow time from being and,
Apocalypse within his fist,
Mill the outlasting eucharist.
In but his beard and all his sins,
From fiery mouth to spindle shins,
John Ruskin, resurrected, stood,
Resumed the gallop of his blood,
Resumed his stare, and all but spoke
When marigold and sifting smoke
His flesh became, and fell, and where
The vineyard of his ribs was bare
Sat Jerusalem in his breast
That seemed Siena from the west,
But Venice east and Sparta south,
And north, on Thames beyond Thame mouth,
O crystal fold of years and shires,
Grey Oxford with her silver spires.
Came now through lilac drenched with rain
An armature of cellophane,
Frail Thomas Peacock wrapped in light.
And Stanley Spencer rose upright,
Who, naked as a swimmer, stood
As best his sleepy body could
Beside his tombstone while his wise
And deep and dark untroubled eyes
Watched the startled, exultant dead
Take flesh of fire in flesh's stead.
Henry Purcell and Edward Horn
In dancing, dashing light reborn,
Thomas and Henry Vaughan who go
In hair as white as Finnmark snow,
And Edith Sitwell lift her hand
To Henry Fillmore's saraband,
And, whistling to the banjo, prance
Stan Laurel in the harvest dance,

And print the dew with silver tracks
Sir Arnold Edward Trevor Bax.
Split lichened antique stone and stout
Sir Thomas Urquhart floated out,
And came, where granite heaved and gave,
Proteus Steinmetz from his grave.
In spiral sheen from eyes to toes
Thin Christina Rossetti rose,
Botticellian and long her hair
Astream unbound on kind green air.
Here rose through parted columbine
The solemn Ludwig Wittgenstein,
And lettered, ivied marble tore
To offer Søren Kierkegaard.
Tall Pumpelly the traveller woke,
Through mullein and mole burrow broke,
Through clay Hugh Miller shyly rose,
Through water can and garden hose,
Dandelions and field shrew's house,
Johannes Brahms and Octave Maus.
Here tossed his coffin lid aside
Black Roger Casement in such pride
He wore for flesh transparent flame
That shivered from his shattered frame.
His bones were water, then were air,
But Casement was still standing there.
This man of light and shadow burled
Was Alan Turing in the world,
This fire on holly after rain,
Admiral Sir Frederick Jane.
O harvest, harvest of such grace
From counterfolded time and space,
Christopher Smart, his brindle cat,
John Martin in his Roman hat,
Boole and Babbage and Bishop Hall
And Mrs Heelis in her shawl.
Through throstle charm, from sundered ground,
The tall Charles Doughty upward bound,

And Hooke the witch on broken knees,
And, choired, the masters of the trees,
Henri and Théodore Rousseau,
Camille Bombois and Jacques Teyssot
And Baron Ensor of Ostend,
John Clare and in his hand that friend,
The only one he could abide,
Who, in his waistcoat when he died,
Went with him to God's splendid house,
His Inniskillin pocket mouse.
And now the brilliant silence broke
And God among the risen spoke,
While bells in rounds, by angels rung,
With iron anthem shouting tongue
A hundred grandsire triples roam,
Shake out, and call their treble home.
That coat of hair Elijah wore
His windy radiant body bore,
And stole of stark archaic stitch
With birds and flowers worked and which
Had once belonged to Cretan Zeus,
And Isaac's wild and brown burnous.
My synagogue at Chartres stands
Within the hollow of my hands,
Athene's church and groves of slim.
Sillima is my seraphim,
Hauterives and Saint Apollinaire,
My painted chapel at Burghclere,
Assisi and Sofia's dome.
Hadschra Maktuba was my home.
At Bethel and at Highgate I
Have burned within the willing eye,
In light as under Tobit's vine
Or deep in Cana's sudden wine,
In quartz and hollyhock and dark
Diktynna of the laurel bark
Or midnight moon upon the wheat
Where Ruth lay still at Boaz' feet,

In leaves at Senlis flaming green,
The visions of my Séraphine,
Hosios Loukas where the light
Within my sanctum falls so white,
Clear and Attic, pure and cold
Upon mosaic blue and gold,
To quince and cypress am I known,
The very scorpions and the stone.
I put my living hands upon
Tetrahedrons Arachne spun,
For foretime here lovesick for there,
Jig, hey, of gnats in shaking air,
Made this mirror of grief and love,
Fine replica of what's above.
I put my fingers down among
Foxfire anatomy and dung,
Unbind, and with immortal breath
Annihilate his magic death,
The double dream infolding man,
The golden world more troubled than
Dark rapture of the sullen dead.
Now, said He, shall I bake my bread.
I put my hands within and meet
Quincunx of seed and hands and feet.
Tassili cow, Basundi thighs,
What made I lovelier than eyes?
You painted me the antelope,
In lurs and pandores carved your hope.
The Solutrian myrtle leaf
Defined in flint your whole belief.
Zophar, Bildad, did you expect
The burning tiger's architect,
Quaternion, stone-hearted men,
Never to wake his own again?
Entuthon Benython break out,
Light from the quick of carbon spout.
Let beryl Golgonooza burn,
Loom and furnace and man return

Within my bowels' very life:
Jerusalem shall be his wife.
From selfish eyes that would not see,
O feet nailed downward to the tree
That smelled the waters of the world,
Atoma mundi have I hurled,
That jot against the tittle split,
Till proton anti-proton hit
And knock the iron world away.
Did not my Herakleitos say
Under the noon Cycladic sun
All is other and all is one?
Now finished time becomes a place.
Time, time was psyche unto space,
And space was time within my hand.
Move near. Like Zacharias stand
In ash of gold and mist of spice
As when he, tending sacrifice,
Upon that snail and tendril plinth
Burned amber gum of terebinth.
Now shall I, that your light abide,
Take mortality from your side.
And blare the trombones on a ground
Of diligent audacious sound
Both Persian dance and B flat prime
Presbyterian four four time,
Viola, harp, and Shaker hymn,
Te Deum from the Cherubim.
Gabriel's shofar thunders out,
Dominions, thrones, and powers shout
Hosanna! Adoremus O
The silver C sharp trumpets blow.

Soldier

ARCHILOCHOS

My ash spear is my barley bread,
My ash spear is my Ismarian wine.
I lean on my spear and drink.

Girl

ARCHILOCHOS

She held
        a sprig of myrtle she'd picked
And a rose
That pleased her most
Of those on the bush
And her long hair shaded
        her shoulders and back.

Thasos

ARCHILOCHOS

This island,
        garlanded with wild woods,
Lies in the sea
        like the backbone of an ass.

Battle

ARCHILOCHOS

When the fight's with those hard Euboians,
No bow-string's whine or snap of bow-notch
Or whip of sling do you hear, but a delirium
Of Ares, sword work and spear sticking,
The tall Euboians famous for their knives.

Fireworks on the Grass

ARCHILOCHOS

[   ]
Back away from that, (she said)
and steady on [   ]

Wayward and wildly pounding heart,
there is a girl who lives among us
who watches you with foolish eyes,

a slender, lovely, graceful girl,
just budding into supple line,
and you scare her and make her shy.

O daughter of the highborn Amphimedo,
I replied, of the widely remembered
Amphimedo now in the rich earth dead,

There are, do you know, so many pleasures
for young men to choose from
among the skills of the delicious goddess

it's green to think the holy one's the only.
When the shadows go black and quiet,
Let us, you and I alone, and the gods,

sort these matters out. Fear nothing:
I shall be tame, I shall behave
and reach, if I reach, with a civil hand.

I shall climb the wall and come to the gate.
You'll not say no, Sweetheart, to this?
I shall come no farther than the garden grass.

Nebule I have forgotten, believe me, do.
Any man who wants her may have her.
Aiai! she's past her day, ripening rotten.

The petals of her flower are all brown.
The grace that first she had is gone.
Don't you agree that she looks like a boy?

A woman like that would drive a man crazy.
She should get herself a job as a scarecrow.
I'd as soon hump her as [kiss a goat's butt].

A source of joy I'd be to the neighbors
with such a woman as her for a wife!
How could I ever prefer her to you?

You, O innocent, true heart and bold.
Each of her faces is as sharp as the other.
Which way she's turning you can never guess.

She'd whelp like the proverb's luckless bitch
were I to foster get upon her, throwing
them blind, and all on the wrongest day.

I said no more, but took her hand,
laid her down in a thousand flowers,
and put my soft wool cloak around her.

I slid my arm under her neck
To still the fear in her eyes,
for she was trembling like a fawn,

touched her hot breasts with light fingers,
spraddled her neatly and pressed
against her fine, hard, bared crotch.

I caressed the beauty of all her body
And came in a sudden white spurt
while I was stroking her hair.

Troop Ship

ARCHILOCHOS

How many times,
How many times,
On the grey sea,
The sea combed
By the wind
Like a wilderness
Of woman's hair,
Have we longed,
Lost in nostalgia,
For the sweetness
Of homecoming.

Old

ARCHILOCHOS

No more does this smooth flesh stand slant and bold
Now that it's withered, and I am old.
It quickens still at splendid eyes,
But its seed bag's dry, and it will not rise.
Cold winds and winter drive us on.

Landlord

ARCHILOCHOS

A great squire he was,
And heavy with a stick
In the sheeplands of Asia.

Prudence

ARCHILOCHOS

Some Saian mountaineer
Struts today with my shield.
I threw it down by a bush and ran
When the fighting got hot.
Life seemed somehow more precious.
It was a beautiful shield.
I know where I can buy another
Exactly like it, just as round.

Strategy

ARCHILOCHOS

Fox knows many,
Hedgehog one
Solid trick.

Morning Report

ARCHILOCHOS

Why should the sea be fat
With my drowned friends?
Why oil the knees of the gods?
Why, why should Hephaistos
The Fire dance his dance
On this splendid face
And feast on these runner's legs
Poseidon the Water has stilled?
To the ecstatic fire we give to eat
This fine body wrapped in white,
Pleasure once of glad women,
Companion once of Ares, War.

Just So

ARCHILOCHOS

It's not your enemies
But your friends
You've got to watch.

Fortuna

ARCHILOCHOS

Fortune is like a wife:
Fire in her right hand,
Water in her left.

Grace

ARCHILOCHOS

As a dove
To a sheaf of wheat,
So friends to you.

Poem: For Lu Chi's Wen Fu *(302 A.D.)*

The fu *is an essay in verse; Lu Chi's is upon the art of writing.* So-shu, *"grass-writing", is the gentleman's individualized brushing of the ideograms;* ming *is "bright". One's heron was taken out to see the plum blossoms in the dawn mist.*

Morning, cushat all a cooing, *so-shu* brusher,
Taking, mantled in mist, the crane out boating,
Looking for plum blossoms, rust in the dawn?
Ming in the black pines, damsons in a smoke!
Ah, skiff-skipper, bonneted and tucked sleeved,
Your hern hen's white as humped snow, but moving,
Han bird, out to see the plum's flower, pleased
Old heron. And you, punter, *fu* artificer Chi,
Word chiseller, line carver, and tight calligrapher,
Who called the heart's heat a bosky dragon
And a marksman archer the heart's precision,
Here's a hierogram for a heron boater's musing:
Ever see a jack wasp drinking at a faucet?
Summer garden's zinnias, Queen Anne's Lace,
Fennel, gentians, sedge grass all around him?
Words, you've said, must bring the proper colors,
And there he is, the waeps, wespe, Old Hesper Bee,
Drinking upside down, the gutta with a core of fire,
Crispy silence while he sips, pulsing with his thirst.
A bandit's soot upon his cheeks, dusk rover,
Lord he is and plunderer, too, of plum blossoms,
Precise carpenter, named for the west star Hesperos,
Rocket and Dame Violet's cousin in vespery things.
Watch the weaver, Lu Chi, at the dripping faucet.
There's a dragon still by crystal, dusk by glare,
Spiralled vigor tense but fixed in meditation,
Your prescribed control for writers at their writing.
Is that what you meant, old Sidney of China?
Out a heron boating in the dawn mist, are you,
Well, add the narrow wasp to your conclusions.

At Marathon

Marianne Moore saluted the battlefield.
Her frail hand at the brim of her hat
round as a platter, she stood at attention
in her best Brooklyn Navy Yard manner,
or as years before she and Jim Thorpe
raised the school flag at Carlisle.
Here in long scarlet cloaks the ranks
advanced with ashlared shields, singing
to the thrashed drums and squealing fife
the pitiless hymn of Apollo the Wolf,
spears forward, horsetails streaming
from the masked helmets with unearthly eyes.
The swordline next and the javelineers,
More red cloaks, Ares wild in their blades.
The javelins whistled up like partridges
flushed in a brake and fell like sleet.
The Persians bored in, an auger of hornets.
The Greeks flowed around their thrust
as fire eats a stick. Wise to the ruse,
the Persians pulled back to the sea
and made hard in their ships for Athens,
which, the Greek army there on the plain,
lay naked to their will, tomorrow's victory.
But the Greeks were there on the morrow
to cut them back. They had run all the way
from Marathon, twenty miles, in bronze.
Two thousand, four hundred and fifty-five
years ago. There are things one must not
leave undone, such as coming from Brooklyn
in one's old age to salute the army
at Marathon. What are years?

The Medusa

is Juno of the Ribbons in gelatin,
little more, as Lyman said to Agassiz,
than organized water, Hegel's brain
in a lace shawl, knit moonlight,
its dome of liquid glass
sealed by invisible sutures,
its spore sacs disguised as eyes
alternate with eyes, testicle eye,
testicle eye, petalwise radiant,
six sexes flowering in six eyes
fringed with pleats thin as wine
down the side of a glass
stitched to the dome with cobweb.
Its confetti of forty legs
hang below, mylar orchid roots,
a silverpoint page of da Vinci
on the purl and meander of rivers
that eddy, curl in countercurl,
like Isabella d'Este's hair.
This anatomy of water
with its crystal bowl of a hat
hung with sexual eyes and optical sexes
is named Medusa by the masters
of naming, Arethusa and Ariadne,
ladies whose fate was in mazes.
It is the Portuguese Man of War,
the sea nettle, the stinging jellyfish.
Builders with baskets of atoms
in the seven days, sticking the protozoa
together, called these humps of slime
bearded with transparent fern
The Electric Lady, Quintessential Venus,
Jezebel in Panoply, Hera of the Tassels.
This gracefullest sphere ringed
and dressed in Isolde hair,
crawfish-shy, improbably intricate,

and by any virtuoso craftsman's word
impossible, is fifty pounds of water
and four ounces of flesh,
is an electricity of convolute frills,
and is transparent. You may see
through it what's behind, a fish
rippled as in a mirror with a warp,
or coral squeezed and stretched
by this lens of fat water. To
copulate it rolls cogwheel fashion
around another which in turn
is rolling around another, eye
looking into eye, seeder into socket.
It is an hermaphrodite and can
if the press is great mate with six
at once and has been known,
what with the sea unsteady and itself so slick,
to shoot from among its fellows
two feet into the air.
It hatches not baby Circes but
anemones, carnivorous flowers,
pomegranates of the ocean which
like their Titan parents are
Venus and Mercury blended.
Headless, they are not beings
but the seeds of beings,
parent, egg, and infant in one,
bones of water, flesh of film.
Their progeny is the ghost octopus
with legs of smoke, the dozen-crotched-
and-eyed Medusa Cyanea,
fire in azure, quick to sting,
a ferociousness of light
in the cold dark of the seas.

Wind's Source in the Bend of the Road

PIERRE REVERDY

a grey dust
in the air
a south wind

on stout wings
dull river sounds
the evening upsidedown

the night wet
as it comes
around the bend

of rough roads
tasting of cinders
and along paths

where you hear
the church organ
its old recessional

making the heart
a pitching ship
and speaking of

failures and hopelessness
when the fires
in the fields

go out one
by one when
eyes are wet

like the grass
when roses shed
we go barefoot

over the leaves
dawn scarcely light
someone is looking

for an address
in an alley
stars have brightened

late flowers topple
across fallen limbs
the dark brook

licks its lips
without opening them
like the circumspect

when the sundial's
sure step edges
another notch along

toward the horizon
the shouting's over
the weather's changed

and I walk
with the sun
in my eyes

all was for
nothing some names
and some faces

I have remembered
everything that happened
in the world

was a holiday
on which I
wasted my time

The Wedding of Ektor and Andromakha

SAPPHO

I

Crying Asia! that famous place,
The messenger came from his dust.
Crying Ektor! the winded runner
Silver with sweat, laughing, Ektor!
Ektor comes from that famous Asia,
From its strange towns with his friends.
They bring home a black-eyed girl
From Theba the high on the Plakia,
The graceful, the young Andrómakha.
They come in the ships on the ocean.
For gifts they bring wrist-chains of gold,
And purple coats and silver jars,
And carved toys incredibly strange,
And things made of ivory.

II

So the runner said.
Quick with astonishment,
Ektor's father shouted for his friends,
And told the coming the city over.
Ilos' boys put wheels to the high carts
And hitched the mules. Wives and girls
Came to stand with Priam's daughters.
Bachelors led the chariot horses;
Charioteers like gods sang commands.

III

A long parade sings its way from the sea.
The flutes are keen and the drums tight;
Charmed air holds the young girls' songs.
Along the way the people bring them bowls
Of cassia, cups of olibanum and myrrh.
Dancing grandmothers shout the marriage song.
Men and boys march and sing to Páon,
To Apollo of the harp, archer of archers,
And sing that Ektor and Andrómakha
Are like two of the gods together.

Horses in Flowers

SAPPHO

Come out of Crete
And find me here,
Come to your grove,
Mellow apple trees
And holy altar
Where the sweet smoke
Of libanum is in
Your praise.

Where Leaf melody
In the apples
Is a crystal crash,
And the water is cold.
All roses and shadow,
This place, and sleep
Like dusk sifts down
From trembling leaves.

Here horses stand
In flowers and graze.
The wind is glad
And sweet in its moving.
Here, Kypris [ ]
Pour nectar in the golden cups
And mix it deftly with
Our dancing and mortal wine.

Vale

SAPPHO

When death has laid you down among his own
And none remember you in all the years to be,
Know, grey among ghosts in that twilight world,
That, offered the roses of Pieria, you refused,
And wander forever in the dark lord Aida's house
Reticent still, with the blind dead, unknown.

Himself

SAPPHO

Down from the blue sky
Came Eros taking off his clothes,
His shirt of Phoenician red.

The Arbor

SAPPHO

He seems to be a god, that man
Facing you, who leans to be close,
Smiles, and, alert and glad, listens
To your mellow voice

And quickens in love at your laughter
That stings my breasts, jolts my heart
If I dare the shock of a glance.
I cannot speak,

My tongue sticks to my dry mouth,
Thin fire spreads beneath my skin,
My eyes cannot see and my aching ears
Roar in their labyrinths.

Chill sweat glides down my back,
I shake, I turn greener than grass.
I am neither living nor dead and cry
From the narrow between.

Anaktoria

SAPPHO

Handsome horses O shiver and admire,
Long ships and symmetries of archers,
But black earth's fine sight for me
Is her I love.

Heart's hunger all can understand.
Did not she up and leave the best of men,
Helen that beautifullest of womankind?
[ ]

And forgot her kin and forgot her children
To follow however far into whatever luck
The wild hitherward of her headlong heart
[ ]

[ ]
[ ]
Anaktoria so far away, remember me,
Who had rather

Hear the melody of your walking
And see the torch flare of your smile
Than the long battle line of Lydia's charioteers,
Round shields and helmets.

Kleis

SAPPHO

They wore red yarn to bind their hair,
Our girls when they were young,
This, or no finery at all.

That, to be grand [ ]
But those labyrinthine curls of yours
Yellower than [ ]

Great overhanging hat of leaves
And the fattest of flowers,
With a snug and perfect snood

Embroidered, Persian, and from Sardis
That [ ] city
[ ]

And Kleis, I do not have for you
That snood stitched in colored thread
You've asked for, but in Mytilena

[ ]
Girls [ ] to have [ ]
If the embroidered [ ]

These Kleanaktida [ ]
You run from [ ]
These memories. We have lost our name.

Hesperos

SAPPHO

Dusk and western star,
You gather
What glittering sunrise
Scattered far,
The ewe to fold,
Kid and nanny home,
But the daughter
You send wandering
From her mother.
[ ]
Esperos, most beautiful
Of stars.

Endymion

SAPPHO

The moon has set, and the Pleiades.
It is the middle of the night.
Hour follows hour. I lie alone.

or:

The moon has gone
To her Endymion,
The Pleiades
Their seven lovers please.

Since Esperos glistened
And the moon rose red,
I have listened
Alone in my bed.

Parting

SAPPHO

Before my lying heart could speak for life
I longed for death. Misery the size of terror
Was in her tears when we unclasped forever.
Sappho! she cried,

That I could stay! Joy goes with you, I said,
Remember what has been, the rose-and-violet crowns
I wove into your hair when we stood so close together,
Heart against heart,

The garlands I plaited of flower with flower
Around your graceful neck, the oils of spices
As precious as for a queen [
[   ]

Deep in the cushions on that softest bed
Where, free in desire [
[   ] tender lovers
[   ].

None [   ] holy, and no [
There was, that we were apart from [
No sacred grove [
[   ].

A Hymn to Artemis of the Strict Observance

For A Chorus of Spartan Girls Dressed as Doves
to Sing at Dawn on the Feast of the Plow

ALKMAN

1

[ ]
[ ]
[ ]
[ ]
[ ]
[ ]
[ ]
[ ] Polydeukes.
Find Lykaithos among the dead,
Enarsphoros the fast runner
Thebros [ ] the violent
[ ] the helmeted
Euteikhes, landlord Areios [ ]
The mightiest of men half gods.

2

[ ] the hunter
[ ] the great and Eurytos
[ ] blind tumult
[ ] bravest
[ ] we shall not go across
[ ] destiny and providence
[ ] oldest of all the gods
[ ] force goes barefoot
Wild heart crowd not divinity
Nor rush upon Aphrodite
Hot to marry [ ] Wanassa, nor any
[ ] Porkos' daughter
[ ] Graces from the house of Zeus
[ ] eyes all love in their looking.

3

[ ] fate
[ ] to friends
[ ] gave gifts
[ ]
[ ] destroyed youth
[ ]
[ ]
[ ] left, the one by an arrow
[ ] marble millstone
[ ] to Hades
[ ] they
[ ] are forgotten
Suffered evil their own hands made.

4

Vendettas end among the gods.
Serenity's against the odds.
But weave and anguish is your thread.
Agido's light I sing instead,
Which is the sun's, and she our sun;
They shine, we cannot tell which one.
And yet I must not praise her so:
One lovelier than Agido
Must have first praise. Choirmaster, she,
Dazzling as when a stallion, he
Runs beside his stateliest mare,
Outshines us all, O no compare!
A race-horse, she, a champion blood
Long-tailed Paphlagonian stud.

5

See how her hair, so thick, so bold,
A long mane of Venetian gold,
Flowers around her silver face.
What figured image can I place
That Hagesikhora shall stand
As if you touched her with your hand?
I'll keep the horse. Then Agido,
Less beautiful, but scarcely so,
A Colassaian filly seems,
Behind her runs and like her gleams
In the Ibenian races. Or
A Pleiades of doves they are,
Or Sirius rising to light
The honeydark sweet summer night.

6

Hold O Sidonian red our wall.
With wrists snakebound we stand or fall.
Our golden, written serpents stare,
Lydian bright bands bind our hair.
We stand, contending, jeweled girls,
Unarmed except by Nanno's curls.
Armed with but our violet eyes,
Ainesimbrota's beauty vies,
That Philylla loves, and Thyakis,
Damareta and Astaphis,
Wianthemis the randy, too,
Klesithera, Areta who
Is like a god, but silver-heeled
Hagesikhora is our shield.

7

Is Hagesikhora our own,
So elegant of anklebone?
As faithful as to Agido!
The gods we could not honor so
But that, O gods, you love her too.
What you mean humankind to do
She does, and brings perfection home,
While I, who sing by metronome,
Ordinary and unaloof,
Hoot like an owl in the roof.
When on Aoti's A we pitch
How flat the Doric counterstitch
O Hagesikhora, unless
You join the ringing loveliness.

8

The trace-horse [ ]
[ ] the pilot
The ship [ ]
More sonorous than Sirens
[ ] who are gods
Against eleven, ten [ ]
Sings [ ]
On Xanthos' waters [ ]
The swan [ ]
Adorable blonde [ ]
[ ]
[ ]
[ ]
[ ]

Hymn to Hera for a Chorus of Spartan Girls

ALKMAN

Around my heart O singing Olympians
[ ] songs
[ ] hears
[ ] of that voice
[ ] a fine song singing
[ ]
Eyes in the honey of sleep half-closed
[ ] take me along, lead me on
Where wildly shall I shake my yellow hair
[ ] my graceful feet.

(lines 11-60 indecipherable)

All go limp when they see her walking,
Unstrung as if by sleep or sudden death,
All empty and delicious in their minds.

But rather than give back my gaze,
Astymeloisa with her crown of leaves
Goes by like a fierce white star that flares
The brighter sliding down the sky,
Like the first green gold of a tree in spring,
Like milkweed down on the wind
[ ]
On long legs striding she walked away,
And in her long wind-tangled virgin hair
The wind-borne grace of Kinyras rode.
[A] stymeloisa against the contenders
[ ] darling would tame
[ ] I choose
[ ] would that, would that silver
[ ]
[ ] could I but see [ ] lovers
But if her gentle hand took mine,
How fast would I fall on my knees before her!

And now [   ] that stubborn girl
To that girl [   ] holding me
[   ] that girl
[   ] grace.

(lines 86-90 are missing)

Night

ALKMAN

The valleys are asleep and the mountaintops,
The sea cliffs and the mountain streams,
Snakes and lizards from the black earth born,
Forest animals and beeswarms in their hives,
Fish in the salt deep of the violet sea,
And long-winged birds.

You and I Together

ALKMAN

My hearth is cold but the day will come
When a rich pot of red bean soup
Is on the table, the kind Alkman loves,
Good country cooking, nothing fine.
The first day of autumn, be my guest.

Epigrams

ALKMAN

I

Boast and brag, such was his fame.
Love You All was his good wife's name.

II

Whoever they are,
Neighbors are neighbors.

III

He was neither a peasant
Nor awkward with fine folk,
Neither born in Thessaly
Nor a shepherd of Erysikhe,
But from Sardis the high.

Imp

ALKMAN

That is not Aphrodite in the ginger grass
But randy Eros batting flowers.
Touch not! Touch not! he cries.

Poem Begun by Ronald Johnson

First one step, then
the other.
A carpet of solid brown
thrashers,
                    or pepper trees
covered with hummingbirds
the day after the equinox
every Amazonian spring —
a shawl of birds.
The world is dressed
cloth upon cloth,
                                  of fire
or light, or thinner still,
imaginary fire and light
of familiar solidity
through which the foot
cannot crash.
And thinnest of all,
the outermost dress
is mirror
so that we cannot see
the sea: it is the sky.
And the sky is a shell
of air.
        Green itself is what
shattered sunlight dances like
there on the leaf
                                  reflected, refracted,
polarized, turned to the left
after its right-hand spin
outward from the sun
which unlike us
is dressed in fire.
The moon is
                        clothed in earthlight,
sunlight, starlight, and

the thickest light of all,
the dark.
"Between Somerford
and Ocksey,"
Cobbett wrote
in the September of 1826,
"I saw, on the side of the road,
more goldfinches then I had ever
seen together:
I think fifty times
as many as I had ever seen
at one time in my life.
The favorite food of the goldfinch
is the seed of the thistle.
This seed is just now dead ripe."
A cloud of sparrows
pulled Aphrodite's chariot
invisible
as the inside of a mirror.

Swan

MALLARMÉ

Girlish, vivacious, and brash afternoon
That lifts with the wine of its wings
From the haunted seasons of yet to be
Summer's blond and Illyrian winters,
Launch the antique swan whose silence began
Under Babylon where the wisteria hung,
When he should have sung in the red pavilions
Passacaglia, toccata, and fugue,
The inward white of radiant space,
Cygnus and Betelgeuse and the Wanderers,
And swam instead but swan, exile and island and
Is now in this utter reality a brilliant ghost,
An archangelical, proud, fat bird,
Ignorant of what the stars intend by Swan.

Swans

JEAN COCTEAU

Upsidedown in their stilted slide
Charming as bathing girls they all
Through tattered shadows listening glide
To the hunting horn's far fall.

On their father's caverned waters
So level they can do their hair,
They the monster's sister daughters
Ignore the hunters' red career.

Light September gold makes up for
Their glances backward and braids unravelling
From combs of shell and necks raised high
To hear the hunting horn's bronze cry.

Beyond Punt and Cush

The leopards of the Dorze are long,
Polka dot, circumspect, and Christian.
Wednesdays and Fridays they fast.
They fast the forty days of Lent.

Their Coptic eyes turn gold at dawn.
Saints with beards and silver croziers
Kneel never so gracefully by a river
As the long Christian leopards of the Dorze.

Shepherds play Abyssinian interludes
On fiddles with two strings and no fret.
Their cattle shamble in a tall red dust.
Leopards watch them from the hills.

Hyenas watch the leopards, slant beasts
Grinning and coughing and hackling their chines.
They are, say the Dorze, not hyenas but
Gentiles in the vesture of carrion dogs.

Scribes of the Nile in aprons of crash
Listed the Cats of Yesterday and Tomorrow
Among those creatures who are noble,
Akeru and Mau, Kherefu, Re and Neb.

And when an apostle came to Ethiopia
Showing the pages of gospels in praise
Of whatever things be true and honest,
Be just and pure and lovely,

We are already of the tribe, the people said.
We implore Mariamne Queen of the Stars.
We walk with God under the acacias,
We and our leopards, in steadfast praise.

Priapos

AGATHIAS SCHOLASTICUS

The ocean is calm, dark as wine.
No wind to edge the waves with white
or comb them with a wrinkling line,
spray them up rocks, sink them from sight.

Two swallows bright in springtime air
fetch straws to plait into a nest.
Take heart, O sailor, from this pair.
Sail to the Syrtis in the west

And to Sikilia. The price
to pay Priapos, if you wish
to get there, is to sacrifice
One gurnard, one red parrot fish.

A Professor at Bordeaux

AUSONIUS

Let us say of you, Marcellus, that Fortune
took you in when your mother threw you out.
Her cold fury drove you to Narbonne
where strangers were kinder to you than your kin.
Clarence kindly gave you his noble daughter,
the hall was full of students when you lectured,
you became known, rich, and promoted.
Then Fortune, liking turns, varied her hand,
perhaps because she saw a weakness in her pet.
I will not join your critics. I merely mention
your sudden collapse. Professor you remain,
I grant the title, justly, for it admits
the half-talented, the glib, and the lucky.

Duino Elegy I

RAINER MARIA RILKE

What eye among the rungs and hordes
of angelkind would turn and find
my long call through the storm of time?
And if one took me in his arms
I would be nothing in that light.
Sweet of beauty gathering in
is fear's beginning: we love it
because our longing stands uncrushed
in the strength of its harmony.
An angel is a fearful thing.
I keep my loud call in my throat
and stop the deep dark of my grief.
Is there any to turn to then?
Neither angel nor brother, no,
and all the animals are wise
to our bewildered stumbling
in the dark of our signs and myths.
What do we have? The hillslope tree,
our walk in the afternoon,
our customary faithful
things remaining year after year.
And the night, there's always the night
with its wind from across the stars
which we can close our eyes and drink.
She's always there, the night, kind witch,
always, if your heart can love her.
Is she kinder then to couples?
They are hidden from each other.
Have you not learned that secret yet?
Unclasp your empty arms and throw
that nothing into breathless space
to quicken a bird's pitch and dip
if your riddance traverse its flight.
Aprils needed you down the years,
and stars waited till you found them,

forgotten days have sought you out.
As you passed an open shutter
a fiddle under ravishment
was surrendering to delight.
Such was our animal faith.
Was your response in proportion?
Were you not worried with waiting,
thinking it prelude, ruining it
with expectations and designs?
Wanting rather someone to love?
What room had you for a lover
with so many overnight thoughts
arriving and leaving in droves?
Yearn, calling to sight those lovers
whose desire filled all their being,
whose power to feel strengthens us,
whom we would almost choose to be,
whose longing was denied ripeness.
Hymn their praise justly you cannot.
The Hero persists. The background
for his splendor was promise
that he would be seen there again.
Lovers, however, are returned
to nature, exiles home at last,
for good, so exquisite a force
released but once to lovers' eyes
Have you taken in the meaning
of Gaspana Stampa enough
to understand that you must long,
like her, for a love that, lost, lasts?
Should not our oldest pains have borne
their harvest by this time? When will
we begin at last in our love
vibrant without our beloved,
be as an arrow to the string,
which breathless in its singing jump
is more than arrow, string, or bow?
To stand still is be nowhere.

Voices. Listen, heart, like a saint
raised into the air by voices,
still kneeling, voices lifting him,
so native to his ears the words.
We cannot stand to hear God speak.
Our ears can bear the aftersound,
the enriched silence full of Him.
A hush, as from those who died young.
Have churches in Rome and Naples
not told you all about themselves?
Inscriptions have made you read them.
Remember the lettered stone in
Santa Maria Formosa.
What do they want of me? Must I
then take the wronged look from my eyes
that obstructs their pure onwardness?

It will feel strange not to be here,
to leave our familiar world,
to leave the roses, their meaning,
things in which we'd placed so much hope,
strange no longer to be cared for
by the solicitude we'd known,
to abandon our given name
like an old toy. It will be strange
never again to feel a wish,
see all arduous knots drop loose.
All will seem random when we die,
hunting hard and gathering up
until we find some lasting sign.
The living draw their lines too sharp.
Angels, we hear, sometimes don't know
the living from the dead. The wind
across eternity confounds
both realms and chimes in the voices
of each.

The early slain, what more
have they to do with us after

awhile? They have been weaned from things
earthly as from their mother's breast.
But we need them, we for whom grief
is the spring of our best efforts,
we need the great secret to live.
Without the dead would we exist?
Is it an empty myth that once
in lamenting Linos with cries
which were the seed of all music,
weeping for a godlike young man,
we first filled death's anguished hollow
with the ringing sounds that help us,
that we must hear to understand?

Duino Elegy V

RAINER MARIA RILKE

Who could they be, these acrobats.
Wanderers, lives briefer than ours,
wrenched by a will since their childhood,
and, can you tell me, for whose sake?
A will that twists them, tosses them,
hurls them, rocks them, spins them upward,
catches them in uncoiling leaps.
As if from a silkier air,
denser than ours, they somersault
onto their worn old padded mat
trod thin, laid down as if to dress
some wound inflicted by the sky.
All but not there, the letter D
of *Dasein*. Presence, being there.

And O around this middle place
a ghost rose blossoms and closes.
Around this pestle or pistil,
snared in its own dust or pollen,
seeded by its own fruit, boredom,
the smile for show, the tedium
of surface without inwardness.
The defeated lifter of weights,
who, grown old, only beats the drum,
whose skin would fit two men his size,
the other dead, perhaps, buried
already. This is the widow.
That young man seems to be the son
of a neck and a nun, so fine
a joining he is of muscle
and virginity.

Suffering
just beginning has long delays
with a kind of playtime in them
before it grips for good.

O you
that drop like green fruit from the tree
a hundred times a day, a tree
that knows spring, summer and autumn
in one whirl, the tumbler's tree.

Often, pausing, a tender look
begins in your eyes, toward her,
your mother, who's seldom tender,
a sweet look that wanders instead
all over your supple body,
lost in its ripples.
A handclap
signals the dive. Before your heart
can feel a throb, there's the tickle
in your heels before the bound
that can start real tears in your eyes
and, unexpectedly, that smile.

Find it, Angel, that healing leaf
and turn a jar to keep it in.
Shelve it with delights yet to come.
Let its flowery label read
Subrisio saltatoris.
Essence of athlete's charming smile.

Ohio

France is my watchlight,
England is my tree,
Spain is my city wall,
My sword is Italy.

Ireland's my strong arm,
Germany my word,
Ohio is my heart's love,
And prophecy my Lord.

Build me a high house,
Angels at the eaves.
Grow me an apple tree
With a thousand silver leaves.

Grow me a pear tree,
a daughter of the sun.
Put yellow pears upon it
And bless them every one.

For Lorine Niedecker

ALKMAN

Three seasons:
summer green with grain,
flowers by the door.

Autumn.
Moon rises red,
cobwebs in the grass,
patience in a star.

Winter. Hard light
from the windows
meets the firelight
on the hearth.

And a fourth,
so brief,
white and wild,
when trees and girls
go mad.

For Cousin Jonathan

Forty salvos upon Anatolian trumpets
a round of girls a line
of long boys in perpendicular light

Orpheus thereupon in his best tassels
and Sunday harp to Apollo
Lord of sunshine and music Great Day

he sang I bring a worker of harmonies
for his crown of laurel leaves
of oak and olive too to sign his service

to song and justice and kindliness all three
and let there come in procession
Archilochos Basho wide-hearted Catullus

Is that Jonathan as in the friend of the psalmist
asked Apollo or as in Swift
Both O Lord of Light made Orpheus his answer

and his words chime with many kinds of music
in the garden of poets he is a thistle
a sunflower a jonquil a John Ruskin rose

he is a walker of hills let his encomium say
a maker of sunprints books and signs
he is a traveler and a guest in many houses

his lines are cunning knots they sting and sing
they echo in the inner ear
they teach the eye to see as in a vision

let him then be praised among the makers
who find and shape
and shaping find and catch us all surprised

For Basil Bunting

Northumbrian master
of number and pitch

honor far sent, a gift
of words only but meant

to be Greek as a curl
on a flat cheek

the coil of white
the Ismene lily

spirals, hound's tail
when his nose is down

snail shell, paper nautilus
wavetop scroll

ear, weather, world
this shape of turning

for light through matter
makes it spin

and all is round, rounding,
atom, sound, space

through its curves, orbits
of Pluto, are long, long

old wheat of Turkestan
stone age *zea*

Pumpelly found
in the clay of an Anau pot

when we had thought
Demeter of Enna

took it from Etna
fire alive in fields, to eat

and gave it to any
who listened with grief

when she asked at doors
had they seen her daughter?

Pumpelly of the golden beard
last of the real Americans

kept waiting in Japan
until the Shogun learned his rank

Smokes a seegar, his man said,
with Ulysses S. Grant

so they placed a rose and poem
before him and bowed flat

learned Russian at seventy
to find the cultivation of wheat

in Turkestan. Crossed China
quoting Confucius for his needs

Great men have been among us
a few are with us still.

Epitaph

ANAKREON

He was a soldier in the wars.
Timokritos. This is his grave.
Sometimes blood-drinking Ares kills
Not the cowards but the brave.

La Vie

ANAKREON

Here *ha!* is Eros blond as gold
throwing his red ball at my head
to make me come outside and play
with a charming girl in embroidered shoes
and she as you might know
is both well-born and from Lesbos too
and tells me that my hair is white
and says *oh!* she loves another.

Spadger

ANAKREON

Your curls in bunches
thick around your slender neck

lie snipped and scattered
bright upon the black earth.

You look like nothing so much
as a nubby big-eyed calf.

And of my grief what is there
to say, at all?

Lady Breeze

ANAKREON

A mare named Breeze belonging to Pheidolas the Corinthian threw her jockey soon after the field left the gate on the track at Elis. She raced on, however, just as if she had a mount, turned at the post, improved her gallop as she heard the trumpet, crossed the finish line first, and stopped, seeing that she had won. The umpires announced Pheidolas the winner and gave him permission to erect a statue of Breeze at Olympia.

Pausanias, *Travels in Greece* VI:13

This is Pheidolas' mare, name of Breeze,
raised in Korinthos of the double dancing floors,
shown here, honor to Kronos' son,
that all remember the splendor of her legs.

Amphora and Daughterleaf

Flowers and Leaves, Part I: 1-20

When light has foundered wild in death
And the wolf has come to love the dog,
The red left hand of the moon upon October
Kindles the savage grass where the children played.
They seemed by day so grave and handsome there
In the uncut wheat, cornflowers or eyes
We knew not which, or hair or sedge.
How the stillness whispered of their cunning.
Jerusalem! sang the oven bird. Ulro, spoke the crow.

Poppies at their knees, autumn in their eyes,
They stole through the wheat so fat, so brown,
As the wild sad odor of leaves steals inward,
A quietness, a gathered hush, a slyness of eyes,
And charm of voices half birdsong rang
Where left-handed honeysuckle wound her spiral
Under the yellow right hand of the sun.
The year is a winded lion, arrows in his back,
Dying, like the sun, in ripened wheat.

Un insecte, monsieur, l'homme n'est qu'un insecte,
Tall as Apollo, casque polled, ringed and chained
Like starlight walking, die cut and resolute of piston,
Wearing the tresour all and riches of Sidony,
Tined of leg as any high-kneed grasshopper, O
Caro, in satiry and fawny, butternut and buck musk.
Let us set Sister Rosetta Tharp to the virginals,
Cry Arashi Ryuzo to the twelve-string guitar
And hear of Venus readily, for in portreiture I saw

Upon a time her figure, naked fletynge in a see.
She was gillyflower, leaf and frond,
Pale where not pink, cinnamon and wild rose,
Still playing with her kitty and her barley doll,
Little Persephatta, millet topped, mama's *cara*,
The holm wood's Cora in her tucked yellow dress.
If at all she strayed from the edge of mothers,
On the eve, say, of the carnival for winnowing,
When the drums were beating and the horns blown,

Or at the carrying of the sparklers and stalks
Through the wild sea wheat along the harbor shore,
To weep the bronze finch the grey hawk tore,
Or rattled the gourds when a boy was grown,
When old men shook on the threshing floor,
It was to wander to the pastures and the goats,
Or far into yellow fields to gather the scattered blue,
Un insecte, monsieur, un homme est un insecte,
Crawling sideways in the wires of a golden beard

And, tilted on a hair warped in curves, clashes
His husks of shins, as tall grass lashes tall grass
In a crisp September. And up out of mist,
On a smoky day, the grasshopper whirrs, where the black
Sticks of the altar fire cast a thin and hazel air,
And widows turn in twisted black from the temple steps.
Parce qu'il s'est flétri et a perdu sa chair,
Guiltie of dust and sinne, clattering on cement,
Unless, O harper in the garden of the world,

The poppy house and the honed knife's terror
Knot into the tangle that cannot grow, that ben
Of beauté crop and roote, for "Thalia speeds
The chrome tip," and a clean spring is a goddess.
"They builded the looms of generation,"
They bore the Miller of Eternity, his grist,
His "snows of doubt," those children
Who in late autumn, in the afternoon,
Played in the rectory yard, clacking sticks,

With the upward arc of the blue swallow
And the downward, shaking flight of the bat
Above them, in the green evening at Doncaster.
They bore England rose and purple,
Bore her from the ash tern stretching his wing
In the shadow of India Company merchantmen,
From the Saxon crosses in blowing yellow grass,
To the empty fields "terribly without nostalgia,"
With a lean clerk from Lloyd's and a cobra nest.

It is not red weather with a *ts'ao ts'o* of wind
Drumming, drumming, nor that the ears forget
The gay *hsia li* Kuang wove into the snow music,
It is the foundering of the light, that distance
In the western blue. The eglantine or ancient rose
Answers the sun, and this tree sweet and high
That flowers white in May. Doves to the windows do,
And the fragrance we crushed in our fingers,
The diminished light, sparrow, persimmon, grace.

She dances, the Demeter of Arp, in the corn.
Twileaf is her daughter she sings from the dark.
And for those eyes that saw, elfskein spellbound,
With Orpheus' and Eurydice's sight, these hills
Valleys groves rocks mountains and towered wall
Designed an antique javelineer asleep,
Swallows in his armpits' nests, wheat for hair,
And under the tangled vine between his thighs
The song thrush cock asleep upon its eggs.

"Would to God," old Blake has copied out in acid,
"Would to God all the Lord's people were prophets."
In this water, in this water the lady Leda
Broke lavender to bathe. Silver minnows
Hang still in the lucent cool, over their shadows,
And flat perches and bream with scarlet dots.
Who this Leda was is dark to know,
And harder to guess the meaning of the swan.
Young Correggio thought her a Grecian girl

Caught so in the make-like of myth
She came as calmly as a happy wife to bed,
Half heeding the putti with the cross-flutes,
Adolescent Eros or his harp. Out of the
Pool rolling in his gait and with lifted wings,
Snow-hump white waddled the urgent god.
Out of "something very like large handfuls
Of lion's mane and silver paper," questioning
His summons, out of the grape cluster

Heaped with figs on the harvest table,
His eyes are morning glories, his bones smoke,
Every joint a fire of stars, each muscle flame
And diamond running, and his heart there
Through crystal ribs, through a flesh of light,
Is a basket of gentians and peaches laced with lavender,
In which two thrushes brood, two robins sing.
I could not quicker come, he says, the pollen
Clouds, acres of sunflowers and dust of sapphire

Were long to cross, wildering the spaces hid in time:
Jerusalem is a woman whose jealous eyes
Look into mulberry forests, her own spread hair,
And she, tower and girl together, lies twelvefold
In the chest of God and Christ and man,
One structure whose blood is breath, is breath.
The acorn and the crooked lightning walk
In this Tuscan lily of a bird, the high humped
Eastern bull, and a man death cannot bite.

Springtime and Autumn

Flowers and Leaves, Part II

I

Brine sand bones wasps hornets bees
Doves of Dione in braces on a bough
Hasp their feet above him in their trees
(Sya and hyacinth lace his brow).

By the white splendor of black apple groves
He beats the drifted dust and ayre,
Rears his salt tongue back, gapes his nose.
His twisted horns wind out of twisted hair.

Time mutes, hollows, tends what value may
Not defect. The briar's carbon, the rose dust;
Notre génération n'a plus de sensibilité,
"Yet a man, with crisped hair," too robust,

Too taut. "Chestnut color or more slack,"
Apuleius rose to wanton hair,
"Wandering gold upon a ground of black,"
The Thesean brisket torqued, the belly spare.

Near the hedgerow (apples red as wine
Hide his maze) upon a wrinkled neck
White curls bunch along a golden line,
A bull's nape dropping down a human back.

II

Through white lathes of sycamores,
Blended dust about our knees,
Came to the shoaling river where
Glare and green light fell through trees,

Knowing after years of what might
Have been, in a better time,
Innocence, that the wiry, tight
Bounding line (this is Blake)

"Of art, as well as of life"
At least defines one's ignorance,
Able to annotate the circumjacent,
To extract gists from experience.

Maiastra in gowan time, in a rage
For spring, the Moldau spilling, cries
A day the mallow's spoondrift blows,
And green shores foam their hawthorn

White against the river's foam. Of laurel
And goats, that burning afternoon,
We talked of people and Jonson and Tymon,
Not "the straine bred out into baboon,"

But the changing, the growing,
Of Domna Maia who shored
In May the annual dead, whose son,
Lean Hermas, led the changeling horde,

Who darces down the haws, is neat in air,
Shakes the quince spray when its tines are
Rain-fired. Dissolved in glare,
Dun fuselage in dusk, her lines are

Contours of Tuscan jugs, maple blades,
The long drop of the banana flower,
Bellies of wasps, ram scrota, spades.
Her sun-through-Yoshino-white craw

Remembers Maia's breast, eyes her Io's eyes.
Her lean song articulates in modes
Alcmena sang. Neither oblivion nor dust
Has touched her lines whose nodes

Are where green learning meets ἀθάνατα,
Where Brancusi meets the perfection of Egypt,
Shepherdly carver, *du bout du monde,*
White frocked amid sheep when he chipped

Her wild body in yellow stone, curved
Forward in a sweep as frore as the hawk's
Stiff but with the pear's tilt swerved,
With a horn's slow bend to its tip.

III

Mademoiselle Brycz, whose subtle eyes
Distinguished *die Sexuellpolitik* succinctly,
Would not countenance Freud, "all lies,"
Kept ἔρος apart from ἄγαπη, distinctly

Defined. *Maman, mon amie si ardemment adore*
Un jeun homm' qui s'appelle Jesus Christ
(Nom anglais?) que, tous les soirs, elle
S'agenouille en essayant de communiquer avec lui.

παρθενία, ποῖμε ἀλοῖς ἀποῖκε; lyre,
Hazel, smoke, iris rimmed with gold,
Thin smoke above bronze strings, and higher,
Profile of Meissener porzelan, nape hair rolled,

Bound in latticed blue, her serenity
Against the baskets of figs and *liknoi,*
The "Hast thou tasted virginity?"
Her song's answer to the blind boy.

All made things engineered not to last;
Styles hold a fortnight, words a month;
Self expression, or whatever, has passed
For verse, for song; all senses altered

To fatten every taste. *D' essere senza*
Eyes, glans, or tongue, serves
To blunt even expectation. *Senza coglione*
We greet the light with wounded nerves.

Dusk in the robin's eye hyphenates
The stark retina and the embellished throat.
Pavanne upon the maple instigates
Delicate amours, almost in asymptote.

Holbein's Henry is reproduced nowadays
From the navel up; the brain,
In disrepute anyway (his testoons
Sold to India after his reign)

— Half a century by, "the Bauds
Betweene Gold and want" had thieved
The coinage from England forever —
Unbalanced by the striped codpiece reeved

Tight by its points, obvious in embroidery.
As animal evolved from animal,
Each head, elk's horns, man's whorled hair,
Took signature, and from each pelvis,

In heraldic tufts, juglans paired.
Appetence, the eye's hunger, roam
In shapes, or give form to time, love
And the intellect are the one honeycomb.

IV

Hast thou seen the difficult coupling of the dove?
Or blind moles a hugging in the dark?
Hast thou seen braided serpents at their love,
Or, midair joined, the breathless marriage of the lark?

Hast thou seen the puffins nuzzle breast to breast,
Hast thou seen the hedgehog mate,
Hast thou seen the bittern booming out his chest,
Or amorous whales, like anvils, conjugate?

The crocodile labors long upon his lady
And, having done, flips his beloved over;
The hippopotamus churns to froth his waddi.
Hast thou seen the chambered nautilus cover?

V

Maiastra

Out of complex hypocrisy (across blue eyes,
The young's honest gaze, bobbing water's
Ribboned refractions shift in plies)
Guileless action comes, but at a loss,

Without, indeed, an aim (raised arms
Bunched a fluting of ribs to low relief)
Unless the human parallel the force that
Breaks the lean-limbed dogwood into leaf.

That the sylvan virtue, all equity,
(Mêng expanding K'ung) was down
Led to juncture, to the clarity
Of jungle against neat underwood. Thrown,

Braced with the strenuous, a girl of parts
Not entirely, any of them, unsuggested
By the time's demands, the argument from hearts
Was involved, but officially, congested

In its flex, root-dead, but unperceived
Until distinction pruned the tangle clean.
This was not our theme, but the clear out-folding
Of form, sunlight caught in a crisp green.

Ucell', in vortice ver, the ash
Of falling winter is timber for the cusp;
Thalia speeds the chrysalis, the chrome tip.
"da Huelsenbeck, da Janco, da Tzara,"

The renovator Picabia studied the co-ed,
Drew her as a sparking plug, T O U J O U R S
Down its flank. Any clearing of the air
Adjusts a focus.

The ignorant young (who have seen
But distraction, not rest, not, alone,
His swimming lift pellucid green
Against the sun's rust on a cheekbone)

Know neither work nor contemplation,
"Born tired," shattering energy,
Neither Pallas nor Eros for teachers,
Prothalamium at death; at birth, an elegy.

The leaf of the fig, black-eyed wife,
Cheek laid to the pied hip of nanny,
Old Billy's musk, all old pastoral,
Horned kids in the goatherd's arms.

Night whistler, do you mind my song?
Daimon of the Neuse, stone or monodist,
Or herm of brass in a Carolina river,
All forms upon the others pun.

Fingers laced with Fortuna's, those
Warding off Hermes' visit in May time,
They recast the bounty, new baskets,
Who know your traffic (and a hard knowledge),

Who have heard your song
In the obvious green
Where cudding goats a summer
Shake their shallow bells.

VI

cumque sua dominae date grata sisymbria myrto

Beauty unexpected
In her eyes
Catches uncorrected,
By surprise,

Concepts entertained and
Petrified,
Breaks 'em unrestrained and,
Clarified,

Gives 'em back in mild reproves —
Tender toss —
The wind, in charitas, removes
Former dross.

(Unoffended by indifference, the engaging smile
A proper twitch, how and in what wise
Can vigor press, except by guile,
Or true affection take encountered eyes?)

Unless thou change or grow with
Willing grace,
Juno's double lilies
For thy chace,

Venus' education
Will remain
Studied affectation;
Apate's chain

Be thy stead for Artemis,
Jove's surmise,
Or give the Graces leave to
Teach thee love.

VII

Hokusai Gwa, kinoye no komatsou 1820

Eyes for bones and bamboo, autumn
Grasses, dipped the cock's soles in red,
Ran it, bantam cobalt and cinnamon,
Up the mulberry paper, said:

"Leaves on the Tatsuta River,"
Pine cones by the hern's breast,
Dragon fly on the chrysanthemum.
All the heart loves, neglect the rest,

Said Chung Ni. Time will not hold,
The indifferent leave no loveliness.
Grasshopper crouches on his gourd;
Agility involves a tenderness.

Bowed double to *The Mustard Seed Garden*,
Studied the cricket, Rihaku, the carp,
The Old Man Mad About Drawing,
The cherry wood under his scorp

Became "a little of the structure of nature,"
Caught in the eyes' wit and unwobbling art.
His hands, restless as mice, were taught
By eighty to execute all creation by heart.

VIII

Mulberries, cedars, and fig-trees
In a Warwick garden, ᾧ δαμάλης Ἔρως,
Landor with a yellow-stippled trout,
πλέξαντες μηροῖς πέρι μηρούς,

Apricots of Tachbrook, "beauty
An absolute equity," Picasso correcting
Puvis de Chavannes with a real horse,
Boy in brown study, protecting

The hard emotion, ὁ Θέος ἐν τῷ παιδί,
From "the ideal." All anguish is
A rancid honey and will soak
Sweetness in, in time.

IX

Kirkwood, Missouri

"And" (the honest old voice intent)
"Got a bill through Congress to print money
"For soldiers' compensation, but the president
"Vetoed it, issued bonds instead.

"The men who could have abolished banknotes,
"(Bryan saved the bankers from 'em)
"Were organized by '94. Forty thousand votes
"(A minority?) gathered by '96."

[And this one imperfection, that she
No longer stands by lilac (did she ever?)
No longer in her gestures conveys an action
Hammered to perfection by her forebears,

That her complex mind, loosed in children,
Drawn to no center, whatever she knows,
No longer takes such bold delight in
The sweet of woodsmoke in his clothes.]

Ignorant of Jackson, Benton, Del Mar,
Barbara Villiers but a costumed whore,
The pappus'd wheat, the bearded herm
Are interesting facts, nothing more.

The total debt of the nation
Is seven hundred billion. Add
A billion interest to that yearly.
"Must we act as if we had

"No respect for the future?
"Chief objective of the American people
"Is to be amused. Human nature
"Among the young takes war for granted."

X

Five years up the Baram, with Penan;
Shakespeare, Spinoza, and Pound
For reading, "health permanently impaired,"
No university wanting him, the sound

Of new learning, of clarity among yatter,
Will not carry to stoppered ears.
Neither money nor repute, but no matter:
Labored for our learning twenty years.

Crouched at the root of his pyrojectory
In the Kohima sandal wood
The fire arc of a Japanese mitrailleuse
Traversed his thighs. He stood,

As always, between blood beating
His belly and malarial agony:
The Antonian web of war and hearts.
His fine hand at the Naga theogony,

At Punan copulatives, at responding
In Lawrencian prose, with a touch of Shaw,
To the live gestures among the *hallucinés*,
"Forced to a barren island," he used his eyes.

XI

This tall woman cracking her knuckles
(Iced tea and Graham crackers under the acacia)
She might rise when the bee and katydid
Cross the dusk on thin wings, knees drawn up,

And say as she smooths away crumbs,
"Those people were wealthy people, and fine,"
Take the tortoise combs from out her hair,
Wring her hands till nine o'clock and sleep.

Would not have nature sex'd and a woman;
Sive natura Odilon Redon can vindicate:
The charcoal spider erects her gibbous belly.
After his saraband, and tup, eats her mate.

Calvert defined Blake, read Landor
And Chapman, engraved a tough line
Fine as Bewick's. (Knowledge rusts
If the mind can't love.)

"Level down, but,"
[O ruddier than the cherry!]
Diogenes Walter Savage wrote,
"Don't they ever level *up*?"

XII

Pages of words, records of *K'an* and *Li*,
A webster wasp in the pine-wold,
The firm, the yielding ("money" and "charity"
For Blake). Three things will not hold:

Light, firm nature, rectitude,
"Then a Sun dyall in a grave,"
In Paphlagonia bina perdicibus corda;
Hok'sai knew the fibres of the wave.

Ignorance, the news came to Nara, is evil;
Not to know, K'ung said, not to know
Cancels the dragons, makes impotent
The mother wit, the energy of men who

"Made gentle the earth." Sweet Nefertari
Led by Hathor — images to seed the air —
Old Walt and Eakins for our pastoral,
And a young born living who hold aware

Clear eyes that not to laurel galls shift shape
Before the startled eyes, or of a sudden end
All longing, but love so ancient clarity
All inconsonance can a twelvemonth mend.

Fire, October, Eyes

Flowers and Leaves, Part IV

O say can you see by the dawn's early
Light peeled birch and folded brier
And western distance in September blue?
Either comedy or incomparable love
Holds our question posed by magic eyes
In a hung mist and red maple of the mind,
Imagination's country and blizzard of gold
And chill Housatonic and the church
In the wild wood, the question neither yes
Nor no but what landlord of this sweet land
Set the hills which so proudly we hail.

In Vivaldi weather of transcendental blue
Trombone winds and a passacaglia of leaves
Bounden love may move, rocks like grazing sheep
Its passage from road to orchard to field,
Conversing of its strangeness in intricacy,
Knots like tendrils, their circuits found
In independent grace and curiosity,
Where one reached the other greeted, a home
And a country and twilight's last gleaming,
Innocence brave and free honoring clarity,
Eyes watching eyes of young and lucid brown.

What, my God! has sound to do with music?
And, and, Illyrian-grandfathered naked rider
Who cut Pentelican marble as if it were snow,
Squared stone, the rock other, stood immortality
As easily in invincible probity as a new ship
In the Medford yards, or new mills at Lowell?
Given man as a golden impossibility,
Manners clean of desperation, bound
In freedom and necessity to apologetic silver,
One and other, bound, the sea shore,
Sea seen from shore, shore seen from sea.

Listen to the mockingbird, who cries Sebastopol!
Between romantic love and capital punishment,
From diamond eyes (they shine just the same)
To the wicker basket, there is little to choose,
And hearts baked in wine or blood a fountain in air,
Marseillaise, tricolor, howitzer speaking Clausewitz,
The bastard En Bertrans and the criminal Vidal
Trussed the changeling in jonglerie and pied stupidity,
The coldest whore they gave a razor for tongue.
O pretty imploration, refrigerator for springtime,
And zero stands the summer's mercury.

Fast falls the eventide; nighthawk, western star
Stir the twilight and the *Wiegenlied* of Brahms,
Wrought for the night was coming, shifted to
Over the mountains toward the west, elf star,
Or lamp of Harmony Twichell Ives darkness
Deepens by the beautiful river, the beautiful.
Abide with me, abide the rocket's glare,
Pretense, menace, the rocket's red glare,
The bombs bursting in air Over! there over!
There shall we gather by the river in the
Land of the brave, home, shall we gather

By the river where inverted reflections variations
Work as in a music of the eye wet girls
Shy and easy, boys glossy and aflame
In full glory reflected; this constitutional
Weather, wildrose red, daisy white, proud
Massachusetts summer Berkshire blue,
All sky and hill in the dawn's early light,
Elms of Pittsfield in Jeffersonian calm,
Republican red, oxeye-daisy white, lifts
Your chin to rippled bunting and sovran stars,
And mounts the starry banner on Matchless handlebars.

Like Ty Cobb walking in goldenrod by the Saluda,
Everything depending on what the philosopher,
Ward politician, unmasked laymen, or pitcher
Nails up on the dashboard as valuable,
Abide with me and baseball cap and Walt Whitman,
A paper butterfly on his finger, buffalo lap rug,
Charles Ives in the shallow Housatonic meadows
Walks with Harmony his wife. We have Thoreau
And the ghost of his flute beyond Concord,
The Alcotts singing hymns by lamplight and
Tannhäuser and his harp on Deutschegrammophon.

Here are the oranges of Hieronymos Bosk and citizens
Naked as lizards conversing among the hot wrens.
Pericarp and pistil, hybrids of pomegranate and cactus
Grow in this garden and Burgundian lutes
Sound the long canzone of Marcabrutz and Machaut.
Stripling and blushet dance impatient to dance;
The boy with the greyhound waist and porcupine hair
Steps to the President McKinley Inauguration March;
Against the turrets of the Smithsonian Institution,
Over the rung silver and shaken gold of Episcopal bells,
The standards flow backwards, the flags, the colors.

In new celerity to time, railroad, wheel; in old clarity
Colonel Christopher Carson; Senator Benton's son
Waxed-chestnut haired, mounted like a monkey,
They have photographed all that, historical sepia
And grief; the horse is ebullience; the blue sergeant,
Spur, flag, wagon, chronometer; Clarence King's
Gneiss and crystal, far into the celerity of time,
Riding westward from sweet Ohio, with bee and bear,
Four thousand humped bison, eagles high, cold,
Over thousand mile long grass fields, a democracy,
The United States of North America, wide.

Greek book, chronometer, General Fremont's deerhide pocket,
The geological expedition dropping, the bugle and horse sweat
Stop the mountain lion, dropping, banjo and captain,
Dropping like the diamond-backed rattler toward water.
Mr Jefferson, if I may offer a suggestion, decent, low,
A particular Bostonian this John Adams, dressed, O my,
Like a circuit-riding judge, supper in a cabbage leaf, sly,
Mr Jefferson, if I'm not mistaken, that tall Virginian
Is our field commander. Mr Washington there, who
Stands with grace and assurance, a certain perspicacity
Of eye. The colony of Georgia has sent no delegates.

Wagner and Haeckel too a century made,
The horn-lifting Parzifal, acanthus spray
In gilt wood, elf sword and dwarf-knit
Dichtung, precision in folly, *Wissenschaft*,
Enigma hatched from accident, shuffled
Chaos from which no seventeen of Blades
Shall ever annoy the prestidigitator,
No Bishop of Dots disclose his polychrome.
Runes and wizardry the dawn carbon ruled,
Centaurs built and benzene hexahedrons; ferns,
Eosauri, petroleum, Hyperion of the Nautilus ear,

Cereus nyktiflora, faunish girls with springbok eyes,
Hyksos kings with beehives for hats, liquidambar,
Yellow bees, William McKinley framed in an oval
Of lycopodium and Quassia, Aphrodita
Or Vagina constrictrix with electrical clitoris,
Under spun copper crystal syrop in her tuck.
Implicit in the concussion of carbon dust
The mind of Charles Babbage that wove algebra
As the Jacquard looms wove flowers and leaves,
And John C. Calhoun waltzing at Clemson,
Grim, Roman of dignity, lightfoot as a doe.

Come up from the fields father, Chickamauga
And the cornet in F and the jumping artillery,
That Constitutional pomp of the inlooped flags,
Eyes grieved by the prudence that suits immortality,
Bivouac and star, brown thrush singing in the brier,
And Peter Shaw of Ohio talking through a foam of blood,
Chickamauga and Seven Pines and Richmond
Send mail to Ohio, to Billerica, to Concord.
Come up from the fields father, here's a letter
From our Pete, and come to the front door
Mother, here's a letter from thy dear son.

In burnt October, brown, in the fourteenth day,
Beyond the fields in the wash of river wind,
The trees, deeper green, yellower and redder,
Cool and sweeten Ohio's villages with leaves,
And apples ripe in the orchards and trellissed grapes,
Late bees in buckwheat drone and the world is rust.
The sky is transparent after rain. Now from the fields
Father comes at the daughter's call. Come to the entry
Mother, to the front door come. Come.
Under parting smoke, quiet with fear, Jackson
To his captains said, Give them then the bayonet.

Fast as she can she hurries, something uncommon,
Her steps trembling, she dares not tarry
To smooth her hair nor adjust her cap.
Open the envelope quickly, O this is not
Our son's writing, yet his name is signed,
A stranger's hand writes for our dear son.
The sentences confuse her eyes, gunshot wound,
Cavalry skirmish, taken to hospital, chest,
At present low but will soon be better.
Sickly white in her face and dull in her head
In wealthy Ohio with all its cities and farms.

Grieve not so, dear mother, the just-grown daughter
Speaks through her sobs, see dearest mother, see
The little sisters are speechless and dismayed,
The letter says Pete will soon be better, will live.
Vigil strange I kept on the field one night,
When you my comrade dropt at my side that day,
Vigil wondrous and vigil sweet, under Orion,
That you die not alone in the summer night,
Vigil of silence, love and death, vigil
Long there in the fragrant silent night.
Autumn and Ohio the vigil keep.

Our dialogue, Jüngling, we speak in two voices.
Here by a lace of ice, our verbs in smoke,
Or barefoot, chucking rocks, many times, two voices.
To Haydn and Charles Ives, to the steel plosives
Of the motorcycle, to the silence of the apples,
Word on word folded, as the wind folds leaves.
How we fare! Jean Calvin my *doctor philosophicus,*
Leading you to observe that the black mills
Of New England and the Saratoga Wallpaper Co.
Please me not so much by their plain handsomeness
As "the children inside chained to the looms,"

Yours the dedicated fanatics of decent tyranny,
Marx to unpocket the rich and shoot the poets,
Freud to re-arrange our guilt; Venus of the idiot eyes
Durch rosiges Licht erleuchtet was the esteemed girl,
Issy Bowman despair of bachelors, Viennese sweetheart,
Throat-clearing *maman* commanding puppet children,
Sigrune und Ritterkreuz her signature.
Man animal we began in Europa's underwood,
Reindeer wizard, hunter, sheathed in Leopard guise;
Ruskin's rose from Flora's thigh rose gold became
And shield his heart half woman stood behind.

Wives, imagine, of the Chelles-Acheul bowmen,
Sworn sergeants of the seed light of the sun,
Women suave as salamanders, tree girls, archers
Under a sunflower yellow sun, their boys
Herdsmen of the mythological horses of Lascaux,
Charging, swimming in grass, muscadine eyed,
Pacing as in the Rasoumovsky Quartets of Beethoven,
Animal people in tmesis between hippanthropos
And the kingwraiths of antelope first of all,
All myth tongues say, witness the Willendorf chalk;
The horse princess nuzzles the queen mare's neck.

This glossolalia of leaves and vortex of wrens
Works beneath our dialogue as the heartbeat
Of battle horses foaming with charge and retreat
Under swordsong and bugle commands in C sharp,
Or, in your reverses from my argument of time
The transformations in carbon of a bounden love
To say her hair a steep falls of combed gold
Drops to her dimpled bottom's adjacence of melons,
Like the erozoic metric of socketed oogamy itself,
Above which the lighter measure of eye dance
And entangled tongues frolics its wild divisions.

With what nonchalance he sees, the boy with pipe,
Tendre comme le souvenir, retina possessed by dream,
Those tough trousers both poem and disguise;
Le crime commence avec le beret mal posé.
Of the poets of the rose, Apollinaire, Cocteau,
The cadre of the citadel when nullity sent
Plunderers to the gates, Tchelitchew, Rimbaud,
He is the Nabi, rose Picasso, *fauve de la ville*,
Clay pipe and charmed vagueness of adolescence,
"Blue-eyed," as Alice Toklas wrote, "and blond,
With irregular features like a sailor,"

René Crevel, one of those vulnerable who exist
Within the windowed walls of a strong style,
Between the *Angstzeit* acrobats of the faubourg
Both *Traumgeist* and transient Ariel kin
And the wild *comédiens martyrs* surviving
The *Sturmabteilungjahren* when time was nausea
And the codicils to existence a sickness
Unto death, who knew that *à la colonie*
Comme dans la marine, c'est le pantalon
Et si tu veux être un homme, tu défends ton froc.
Bach *Handschrift*, pipe, lemons, antique head.

Summer yellowbird who *tchea tchea* flutes,
Teche wiss, where shall, where shall, could
We plunge as the unconverted crow
Despairing up the wilderness pine, shall
We gather by the river early in the morning,
Shall we gather by the river? It is
The oven bird with the C sharp embellishment.
Faded the garden, Gordon Coogler; broken
Sift the leaves from the china grove;
Hollyhocks are down, that grew by the rocker;
Flown the speckled thrush, gone the dove.

When Francis Fant in Silverbrook is laid
And an old she mouse bolts in the corn
With all her young hanging at her teats,
And sheep with snow crumbling on their backs,
And the gipsies eat the roasted hedgehog
By "a deep, ancient stone pit full of trees,"
We take our bearings in nostalgia, from
Samuel Palmer whose mind was a foam
Of moonlit cloud, half vision from Bunyan,
Half poem of Blake, dreamed of a book
Where his drawings of "many autumns, many springs"

Faced Coleridge's poem of oak and raven,
And found in vision limbs like Merlin's knees,
Polydactyl hand in air, Tchelitchew's
Tree with knuckles from before the flood.
A harp this tree and a world this tree,
Syntax of Darwin, Roentgen, and Ovid,
Scuppernongs or golden eyes, leaf-hollow light
Or the infant Charles Lamb a ghost of round shadows,
Children like lights under water, faces tight with sleep,
Here a girl white as the knees of Elynittria,
Rose-petal eyelids, rose-petal lips, tranquil anguish.

This civilization of nymphs like trees in flower,
These figures in blue wool and gold wire,
How long can we imagine their eloquence
Beside Charles Sheeler's locomotives, for hunters under
Acorn ceilings, Giuliano once, leaf hat, flowered coat,
L'éphèbe en blue jeans astride bicylindrical fire,
Birmingham Small Arms cycle climbing the pit wall,
The mind easily Geometric Period infantry corporal,
The heart voiceless, inept, as free of the body
And its leopard engine as music from instruments;
The sincerity of carburetors, the insolence of cats.

The Victorian interior containing Freud,
Velvet walls, Persian tassels, maps of Sinai,
Hang in our considerations, mirrors of water,
Venetian reflections in a corrected lantern slide.
Here, speaking of lions and the prophet Daniel,
A golden carp in an archbishop's confection
Addresses an octopus smothered in lace, saying
That the Trojan-thighed sailor blond and tall
Who has a butterfly tattooed on his foreskin
Needs to decorate the quotidian with style,
Much as the stripper shellacs her teats.

The cat of Pierre Loti, *Hippolyte on l'appelle.*
A sardine of paleological silver the great artist
Gave him when he sat for his portrait, aromatic
And with the *soupçon* of *huile d'olive* about it,
As was proper, whose family reached back
To Nilotic tax collectors in porcelan wigs,
To the bee gums of Beersheba, Akkadian hotels,
(A cousin removed was friend to Mr Smart the poet);
Leo Alektor kept the high gates at Mycenae.
Quite Hebraic, the family tree, rich in detail.
But we are companion to Monsieur Loti.

The cat of Pierre Loti are we. We are civilization.
Our tribe has resided beyond the borders of France.
Mr Rousseau, master in the modern manner,
Has depicted us in forests of flowers, inquisitive
As catfish, intelligent as Miss Gertrude Stein.
Under starlight we have sniffed the desert arab;
Aztec vegetables and Perelandrian trees
Have been our precincts, and the gardens of Tchad.
But in *footballeurs* idiotic with motion
We take our delight, in Gruyère and sincerity,
Innocence, *bicyclettes*, Apollinaire, industry.

Nyssa Sylvatica in a wilderness of wallpaper
Bore her prognathous beauty with Beardsley's poise
Till Dante Rossetti or his complement Jack the Ripper
Brought her in a compound of odors, apple blossom,
Burnt almonds, to narcosis, death, or stupor.
Manchester another Pompeii, perpetual soot,
White moths born black in Darwinian metamorphosis,
Calendar and age *Träume von Hysterinkern,*
Spring, influenza and tuberculosis; black snow;
Wasps carrying orchid pollen traversed in iron dust;
Butterflies took clover brides in a storm of ash.

Dextra victrice conclamantes salutat.
When the barbarians came, swords on their backs,
Carrying their gods in their arms like paralytic children,
Saint with lamp kneeling before a dogwood nymph,
Prophet asleep and his lion asleep beside him,
Our tongues placed on the frozen axe-blade
Were welded by the heat of the ice to the ice of steel;
Colder fire can you come upon, young Erewhonian,
When clarity of heart can ignite marble stone?
Blushet loving banjos, pussy, and motorcycles,
Beauty has no style and honor but one home.

Beyond the virgin blossom, motherleaf, amber berry,
Leaf transmutes to flame; October Chocorua
In the land of maple, burning rampart in mist;
O say can you see by the dawn's early light
What so proudly we hailed at the twilight's
Last gleaming? Whose broad stripes and bright
Stars, through the perilous fight over
The ramparts we watched were so gallantly
Streaming! And the rocket's red glare, the bombs
Bursting in air, gave proof through the night
That our flag was still there! O say

St Gaudens' Rider with Presbyterian face
And anthem eyes, calm as the Parthenon horsemen
On your mount with tail curled like water,
Does that star-spangled banner yet wave over
The land of the free and the home of the brave?
On the shore dimly seen through the mists
Of the deep where the foe's haughty host
In dread silence reposes, what is that
Which the breeze over the towering steep
As it fitfully blows now conceals, now discloses?
Now it catches the gleam of the morning's

First beam, in full glory reflected
Now shines on the stream. It's the star-spangled
Banner! O long may it wave over the land
Of the free and home of the brave.
Time the conflagrator and the lords of dust
Who tilt all balance, all sharpness blunt,
Have burnt the drummers and the leopard-skin drums
Whose honor they could not reach, and grace
With asbestos eye still walks in flames;
The Pittsfield boys at Seven Pines and the Wilderness,
Blood in the eyelets of their high button shoes,

Were not conscripts merely and volunteers.
Can you see, beyond kylix and amphora,
Plumb in blue pleats, her intelligent grace,
The thoroughbred girl in Sappho's poem,
Whose rocket hair hangs like light down her back,
Speaks, as flowering tree to slender oak,
With words like stars, responding to his speech,
The freeman; burned both; an ignition of laughter
Their talk seemed to the staring poet, burned;
Beauty in the fire of time falls like rockets,
Time the beauty of change begotten of fire.

Scrub oak and shale of Carbon County
Or Mytilene in spring, folded like the lighted dove,
Light hovers where fire encounters fire,
Intelligence facing beauty like a comet on a throne;
O thus be it ever, when freemen shall stand
Between their loved homes and war's desolation,
Blest with victory and peace, may the heaven-
Rescued land praise the Power that has made
And preserved us a nation. Then conquer
We must, for our cause it is just, and this
Be our motto: In God Is Our Trust,

And the star-spangled banner shall wave over
The land of the free and the home of the brave.
Tree flowered into stars, first stars of twilight
Star flowers gather to flower stars; night's blue
Sifts into the sunset's blood and snow.
O say can you see by the dawn's early light
What so proudly we hailed at the twilight's
Last gleaming? Whose broad stripes and bright
Stars, through the perilous fight over
The ramparts we watched were so gallantly
Streaming! And the rocket's red glare.

1880

From the Hebrew of Harold Schimmel

For L.Z.

learn my head to take
the palm's sprung green hair
from the seriousness around it
the black pine's green shadow
the green spruce's yellow clumps
palm flag of my revery
that you enjoyed the winter
were wild about July August
September ripening in the sun
You do not see me
in fact I'm not here
she said when I saw
indeed but a body's echo
mounting institutional stairs and I
imagined all the lively rest
sifting what I had seen
from the day's drowned images
the task bending my neck
we'll meet sometime she said
touching my shoulder from behind
first room under the entrance
on Samuel Klein Street under
the terrace the afternoon sun
came from an army camp
behind David Marcus touched me
in bed warmed my midriff
until I found drums remote
in my ears intimate pulse
my penis lifted and nodded
with a rose dip like
a Muslim in his mosque
car trunk full of clothes

changed several times a day
old clothes doffed at stops
on slopes by the sea
in sudden rain day's hours
in accent slant on time
evening the drinks and cigarettes
across a line of palms
each palm like a man
his character wind lifts raises
dances their bodies we dance
her shoulders: their abrupt fall
soft bone to worked biceps
forearm masculine with father's watch?
father's father's watch is it?
square masculine of flat gold
dull on her straight wrist
and I the direct hands
and I the finger's skin
with the gold wedding band
hay's yellow in a field
a long rural stone house
built in the nineteen twenties
bright glare on tin roof
road winds as if Maine
Arab boys walk to work
in ironed clothes Indian file
they do not look at
the Hills of Moab landscape
nor the Dead Sea slopes
nor at the private car
passing at show off speed
when I returned last year
an old Jew in Talbieh
was beating an olive tree
to knock down the fruit
on public property I knew
then that all was well
dust on leaves as humility

a taste in the mouth
of poverty in the fifties
empty lots brought me back
the happiness of that time
horses in the German Colony
the orgy took place as
planned six hours with a
logical parting we could know
ahead from the slight askew
we summoned up for ourselves
need without any other urge
and without peaks of lust
why didn't you come inside?
I did come inside her
OK then! it's all right!
for the record I thought
around her nipple I circled
a finger wet with saliva
thinking and for her pleasure
and then back and forth
with the tongue and all
this to calm her *you!*
you and plans you and
arrangements! and in the end
we examined like real-estate agent
and his client crooked rooms
humpback doors where I stood
near the leaning kitchen wall
to wake her we go
to the roof and come
down again with a poem
blinded now by lime's whiteness
the land is diminutive under
the blue above that covers
a tar film the stain
on my page is shadow
of bird flight the red
in my eyes is blood

I went up to wait
out my laid plan's end
brain molten in familiar heat
tied his donkey Yishai Street
and said the Afternoon Prayer
washed hands in open hut
reddish sidelocks like his beard
dappled grey and eyes blue
like Holiness Hills Tammuz skies
when the sweet kerosene man
appeared first in Mea Shearim
on top of his wagon —
made *Tishah-b'Av* for his parents
I wanted to say just
a moment ago that I
remembered above all my forefinger
knuckle in her mouth for
long hours of an evening
with a teller and we
didn't listen to the Pacific
Ocean which was also there
cold after awhile we covered
ourselves by the picture window
with the blanket she wanted
a flag unfurling in wind
a ship's Saint Mark's lion
an Elephant Ear's leaf unfurling
like a young man stretching
tall and deliberate in sunlight
through a square basement window
square on his sleeping back
making his body dream light
his body spill its seed
I got a kerosene stove
from Dennis who got it
from an English boy *primus*
from Raymond who warned me
against romantic dark Yemenite girls

in allusion to family encampments
with the teacher's college student
I soon stopped fast enough
a folding table soft enough
brown cardboard and folding chair
roof such that my lamp
and cooperation of my heart
both together warmed the room
patterns she came to me
on an afternoon that summer
you really do devour me
she said of the concentration
of my hand's wandering attention
we join feet to feet
limb to limb like cats
who learn to sleep outside
I'll always have to go
and slipped suddenly from something
too clear in my glance
batsheva entices a bee's siphon
an immaterial group of stars
hung downward in a circle
of dream breast the bees
close in on the wall
feel the stone the echo
of sweetness on their tongues
and rest when they rest
on meaty leaves dark green
in their drunkenness they reach
windowpanes nothing to help them
now I read signs when
he removed glasses horizontal on
the floor and she lay
in middle ground between us
the invitation was clear but
how was I to know
a generation older she took
me by the hand and to

her room and to bed
made up with white sheets
my friend in the living
room on a Persian carpet
how was I to know
sweet basil in organic fertilizer
grew in a chickenfeeder's furrow
near five vine leaves tomato
plant cherry variety and curled
parsley a gift from Motsa
back to Talpiot in flower
pots from Bethlehem grows on
our balcony on Jordan Street
with climbers green lizards *spoiling*
of sun and of water
if the phone rings we'll
say it's late for travelers
who just arrived and speak
like children and adults together
about yesterdays yet to come
meanwhile I wrote him about
a journey into unknown parts
so that he can return
home with a clear head
the sooner as they say
the better for us all
what *does* fill you when
nothing fills you? you and
the bottle you and good
hearted grass you and the
eyes eyes that lead you
and take you by the
scruff from place to place
as if you didn't see
enough of all those things
seasons' breasts your heart's trees
suburban alleys their sweet sadness
room's space was world's space

the world's room was here
under my hand and all
this undulation after the deed
and all this remembrance that
accrues and makes of itself
sheaves in the field what
you felt in the wide
meadow of your past's remnants
was under my hand my
thighs behaved like a hand
a forearm an eye's pupil
noise of pages in light
wind like sails and water
racing beneath a blue reflection
which is reflection which reflected?
I am the fish's head
lifted to a scudding cloud
Tiepolo I grabbing a place
near a *piece* spread there
the Gods toss peanut papers
olivepits and Scholem eighty-three
said *that's the last time*
you'll see me and kissed
her then mouth to mouth
and circled her *baggy pants*
embroidered blouse with midway eyes
the writing table promised her
will come at her return
to the Land at midnight
he was banging his books
dust clouds rise on Abarbanel
excellent green basilicum dents like
fender of a smashed car
light beneath rub and free
the smell keep it low
Duomo well set on piazza
near a bend of river
Gioia! written on its wall

which is to say love
you felt yourself giving her
who came from distant grief
an offering of wild flowers
low clouds and fog cross
the morning city with you
highlights there in Salame Circle
because the dew is falling
making windshields and car windows
halfblind as a blinkered horse
everything races in lighted blue
but the old man's gone
and the young man too
sitting together in the park
night near the Pacific Ocean
storming there and roaring there
under our neighbor's complex floodlights
my knuckle in her mouth
wet chewing biting with attention
above and beyond all that
happened under the communal blanket
all those feet and hands
bodies joined in great darkness
free in my life's April
immune to worry the eye
not yet expert in danger
saw its young self surprised
by that high sweet presence
whose goodness like a god's
so stunned my sensing soul
the archer of her eyes
gave my liberty to her
Interlock like a Swiss town
ski resort or like an
American sock that doesn't easily
fall apart so she described
me *you'd like to be*
an octopus and when I

exaggerated in the eating of
a right ear she made
a sound that's translated *come*
come! and I begged forgiveness
and changed from deep thrusts
with my tongue below above
mouthsmouths *let 'em know it!*
Dennis is connected with goats
that circulate between his house
and my room I got
it as an inheritance like
from a girl I knew
at Hampstead Garda Arles Collioure
she left me a collection
of things she received from
her collection of men a
terrible painter with a heart
too large for art so
I picked lemons pomegranates and
figs she picked before me
my garden woman and plants
you lack just at sundown
a little water after morning's
overflow and the wilting afternoon
with sympathy and concern I
fill the kettle and pour
see it's all your hands
by which the withered revive
I don't like my job
let the provider be God
with his hands wide open
a good journey till now
this journey of the years
this tree of time rooted
in childhood lifts you standing
opposite a mirror of kin
examine your face to learn
what you learned in encounters

with yourself and the world
there's the *stable* of you
and the world Rilke's Schimmel
whinnies in a present field
I would find a formula
to allow my complications I
would find an appropriate metaphor
for a connection of eyes
for a longer time caught
and who in any case
rules over eyes? and who
can prevent the connection eyes
heart? as they warn us
in *Hear O Israel* ask
and after your eyes what?
the scratch a little above
the wrist reminds you of
a well planned evening when
hands on my backside as
I enter to convey mutual
understanding the whole thing might
have been different but by
chance took place in an
apartment with a Persian carpet
and on fat upholstered chairs
and in the summer too
you woke with love to
kisses and kisses and she
woke in the corridor announcing
the manner in which I
woke sharp straight pins into
air of the tender day
to whom is she faithful?
and for what? she gathered
love and loves like Diana
arrows you *can't any more*
you *just can't any more*
not I am responsible if

I'm a little in love
with her not by power
of thought and not from
anything else *we have nothing
in common* I keep repeating
as the tie continues high
nervous local voice and a
bourgeois sense of dress and
pride in make-up leaning toward
fame and the names all
this foreign and the body
a brother's body naked to
the line of black pants
in the evening air and
across from her ankle extended
resting on a garden chair
in which a friend sits
the entrance into gradual darkness
on his chest which darkens
without feeling cold spoke of
a blood relation a wall
dividing between bed and bed
a thin division and synthetic
the crazy hours between nothing
and nothing in which nobody
calls you *come to sleep*
and also to something else
not more stimulating and you
on a painful left heel
go fill the Duralex glass
with cold cognac and write
short lines in 2H pencil
public manifestations of a certain
belonging threatened the peace at
home domestic sex increased and
grew wiser in surprising forms
morning woke us to mutual
smiles that I overcame with

the order of the day
and the unsensual woman who
plays love from the head
love leads and the light
taps hit the bull's eye
right clothes and wrong clothes
all the years of innocence
and their exaggerated price how
much suffering you have caused
the companion inside you turned
your back on psychology didn't
catch a call or agreement
you lay on the floor
of a cool apartment good
street didn't know that he
and she are horizontal as
lines between heaven and earth
invited you you spoke in
hints you somersaulted rose fled
backstreets yards fields empty lots
you cross a path between
dry thorns yesterday's paper alive
in wind by your foot
rocks cut off (from their
place?) tan black of a
fresh fire yellow straw of
the season tomorrow's chaff ascents
and descents according to what's
under over friable rich earth
we exchanged clothes love of
the whole of humanity approached
love for a certain shirt's
cotton we met in friendly
words and in the bathroom
of a strange familiar house
come in she said standing
in embroidered panties one leg
raised to step in or

out and my tongue stuttered
sorry and I retreated into
the living room's sanctioned mess
the color of the liquid
twisting like a long tear
the length of her knee
I imagined light orange like
hardening tears of an almond
tree from which hard amber
this sticky adhesion I tasted
from my bones outward to
the dancing on my skull
but nevertheless I didn't come
the guff of sex manuals
touching of toes under tables
across darkness the sharp sense
as if the tendril wanted
to be all the tree
a previous longing led us
to the moment and will
how does the universe absorb
the general noise without excitement
from the wing beat of
the children of the air
to the wheels of buses
Leyland gears uphill a Mercedes
thrusts at changing traffic lights
hold on said the driver
of the new bus insects
reply pines in their sway
answer hammers gunshots sudden stops
the wail of a cat
on the knees upright half
unbuttoned all the positions tie
us to the ground and
to the earth beneath find
our cocoon and you have
found the place of the

lost contact violin and piano
wrapped us in our touch
I guided my head with
my hand to places I
did not know cushioned in
a soft density of down
one understands Cavafy whose day
in day out was erotic
encounters in hallways eyes drawing
near on the other side
of doors of open shops
hands hesitating and the footfall
overlaying another alley after alley
neighborhood to neighborhood and voices
in restaurants libraries behind pulled
shades the body's voice only
the mirror knows who lusts
Otello of Rossini envious black
man kills to the plick
of the harp which Verdi
learned from goes on and
on with pleasing moderation as
the evening passes from quiet
with a shudder to hot
hot who enjoys more the
sucking of nipples? each chair
gets its turn no chair
has the right to be
jealous as democracy reigns after
the splendor of Venetian evil

Comments

DIOGENES

1

I have come to debase the coinage.

2

All things belong to the gods. Friends own things in common. Good men are friends of the gods. All things belong to the good.

3

Men nowhere, but real boys at Sparta.

4

I am a yapping Maltese lap dog when hungry, a Molossian wolfhound when fed, breeds tedious to hunt with but useful for guarding the house and the sheepfold.

5

No one can live with me as a companion: it would be too inconvenient.

6

It is absurd to bring back a runaway slave. If a slave can survive without a master, is it not lawful to admit that the master cannot live without the slave?

7

I am a citizen of the world.

8

We are not as hardy, free, or accomplished as animals.

9

If only I could free myself from hunger as easily as from desire.

10

Of what use is a philosopher who doesn't hurt anybody's feelings?

11

Demosthenes is a Scythian in his speeches and a gentleman on the battlefield.

12

The darkest place in the tavern is the most conspicuous.

13

I am Athens' one free man.

14

The porches and streets of Athens were built for me as a place to live.

15

I learned from the mice how to get along: no rent, no taxes, no grocery bill.

16

Plato winces when I track dust across his rugs: he knows that I'm walking on his vanity.

17

How proud you are of not being proud, Plato says, and I reply that there is pride and pride.

18

When I die, throw me to the wolves. I'm used to it.

19

A man keeps and feeds a lion. The lion owns a man.

20

The art of being a slave is to rule one's master.

21

Everything is of one substance. It is custom, not reason, that sets the temple apart from the house, mutton from human flesh for the table, bread from vegetable, vegetable from meat.

22

Antisthenes made me an exiled beggar dressed in rags: wise, independent, and content.

23

It is luckier to be a Megarian's ram than his son.

24

Before begging it is useful to practice on statues.

25

When the Sinopians ostracized me from Pontos, they condemned themselves to a life without me.

26

Aristotle dines at King Philip's convenience, Diogenes at his own.

27

When Plato said that if I'd gone to the Sicilian court as I was invited, I wouldn't have to wash lettuce for a living, I replied that if he washed lettuce for a living he wouldn't have had to go to the Sicilian court.

28

Philosophy can turn a young man from the love of a beautiful body to the love of a beautiful mind.

29

When I was captured behind the Macedonian lines and taken before Philip as a spy, I said that I'd only come to see how big a fool a king can be.

30

A. I am Alexander the Great.
B. I am Diogenes, the dog.
A. The dog?
B. I nuzzle the kind, bark at the greedy, and bite louts.
A. What can I do for you?
B. Stand out of my light.

31

To live is not itself an evil, as has been claimed, but to lead a worthless life is.

32

They laugh at me, but I'm not laughed at.

33

Great crowds at the Olympic games, but not of people.

34

The Shahinshah of Persia moves in pomp from Susa in the spring, from Babylon in the winter, from Media in the summer, and Diogenes walks every year from Athens to Corinth, and back again from Corinth to Athens.

35

I threw my cup away when I saw a child drinking from his hands at the trough.

36

Go into any whorehouse and learn the worthlessness of the expensive.

37

We can only explain you, young man, by assuming that your father was drunk the night he begot you.

38

Can you believe that Pataikion the thief will fare better in Elysion because of his initiation into the Mysteries than Epameinondas the Pythagorean?

39

One wrong will not balance another: to be honorable and just is our only defense against men without honor or justice.

40

To be saved from folly you need either kind friends or fierce enemies.

41

Watching a mouse can cure you of jealousy of others' good fortune.

42

There is no stick hard enough to drive me away from a man from whom I can learn something.

43

Eukleidos' lectures limp and sprawl, Plato's are tedious, tragedies are quarrels before an audience, and politicians are magnified butlers.

44

Watch a doctor, philosopher, or helmsman, and you will conclude that man is the most intelligent of the animals, but then, regard the psychiatrist and the astrologer and their clients, and those who think they are superior because they are rich. Can creation display a greater fool than man?

45

Reason or a halter.

46

Why Syrakousa, friend Plato? Are not the olives in Attika just as toothsome?

47

Plato's philosophy is an endless conversation.

48

Beg a cup of wine from Plato and he will send you a whole jar. He does not give as he is asked, nor answer as he is questioned.

49

Share a dish of dried figs with Plato and he will take them all.

50

Grammarians without any character at all lecture us on that of Odysseus.

51

The contest that should be for truth and virtue is for sway and belongings instead.

52

Happy the man who thinks to marry and changes his mind, who plans a voyage he does not take, who runs for office but withdraws his name, who wants to belong to the circle of an influential man, but is excluded.

53

A friend's hand is open.

54

Bury me prone: I have always faced the other way.

55

Raising sons: teach them poetry, history, and philosophy. Geometry and music are not essential, and can be learned later. Teach them to ride a horse, to shoot a true bow, to master the slingshot and javelin. At the gymnasium they should exercise only so much as gives them a good color and a trim body. Teach them to wait upon themselves at home, and to enjoy ordinary food, and to drink water rather than wine. Crop their hair close. No ornaments. Have them wear a thin smock, go barefoot, be silent, and never gawk at people in the street.

56

In the rich man's house there is no place to spit but in his face.

57

The luxurious have made frugality an affliction.

58

I'm turning that invitation down: the last time I was there, they were not thankful enough that I came.

59

When some strangers to Athens asked me to show them Demosthenes, I gave them the finger, so that they would know what it felt like to meet him.

60

A choirmaster pitches the note higher than he knows the choristers can manage. So do I.

61

Go about with your middle finger up and people will say you're daft; go about with your little finger out, and they will cultivate your acquaintance.

62

For three thousand drachmas you can get a statue, for two coppers a quart of barley.

63

Masters should obey their slaves; patients, their doctors; rivers, their banks.

64

Against fate I put courage; against custom, nature; against passion, reason.

65

Toadying extends even to Diogenes, I say to the mice who nibble my crumbs.

66

Even with a lamp in broad daylight I cannot find an honest man.

67

There are gods. How else explain people like Lysias the apothecary on whom the gods have so obviously turned their backs?

68

You can no more improve yourself by sacrificing at the altar than you can correct your grammar.

69

We are more curious about the meaning of dreams than about things we see when awake.

70

Pilfering Treasury property is particularly dangerous: big thieves are ruthless in punishing little thieves.

71

It is not for charity but my salary that I beg in the streets.

72

Had to lift its skirt to see whether man or woman had stopped me to talk philosophy.

73

I pissed on the man who called me a dog. Why was he so surprised?

74

Pitching heeltaps: the better you are at it, the worse for you.

75

You know the kind of luckless folk we call triple wretches. Well, these professors and others of that kidney who long to be known as famous lecturers are triple Greeks.

76

The ignorant rich, sheep with golden fleeces.

77

The athlete's brain, like his body, is as strong as that of a bull.

78

Love of money is the marketplace for every evil.

79

A good man is a picture of a god.

80

Running errands for Eros is the business of the idle.

81

The greatest misery is to be old, poor, and alone.

82

The deadliest bite among wild animals is that of the bootlicker; amongst tame, that of the flatterer.

83

Choked on the honey of flattery.

84

The stomach is our life's Charybdis.

85

The golden Aphrodite that Phryne put up at Delphoi should be inscribed *Greek Lechery, Its Monument*.

86

A pretty whore is poisoned honey.

87

If, as they say, I am only an ignorant man trying to be a philosopher, then that may be what a philosopher is.

88

People who talk well but do nothing are like musical instruments: the sound is all they have to offer.

89

Aren't you ashamed, I said to the prissy young man, to assume a lower rank in nature than you were given?

90

Be careful that your pomade doesn't cause the rest of you to stink.

91

Why do we call house slaves footmen? Well, it's because they are men and they have feet.

92

What lovers really enjoy are their spats and the disapproval of society.

93

Beggars get handouts before philosophers because people have some idea of what it's like to be blind and lame.

94

If your cloak was a gift, I appreciate it; if it was a loan, I'm not through with it yet.

95

Why praise Diokles for giving me a drachma and not me for deserving it?

96

I have seen the victor Dioxippos subdue all contenders at Olympia and be thrown on his back by the glance of a girl.

97

To own nothing is the beginning of happiness.

98

Every day's a festival to the upright.

99

Why not whip the teacher when the pupil misbehaves?

100

I had my lunch in the courtroom because that's where I was hungry.

101

It is a convenience not to fear the dark.

102

Discourse on virtue and they pass by in droves, whistle and dance the shimmy, and you've got an audience.

103

After grace and a prayer for health, the banqueters set to and eat themselves into an apoplexy.

104

To a woman who had flopped down before an altar with her butt in the air I remarked in passing that the god was also behind her.

105

At Khrysippos' lecture I saw the blank space coming up on the scroll, and said to the audience: Cheer up, fellows, land is in sight!

106

We have complicated every simple gift of the gods.

107

Make passes at you, do they? Why, then, don't you wear clothes that don't so accurately outline what they're interested in?

108

After a visit to the baths, where do you go to have a wash?

109

I've seen Plato's cup and table, but not his cupness and tableness.

110

If you've turned yourself out so handsomely, young man, for men, it's unfortunate; if for women, it's unfair.

111

A blush is the color of virtue.

112

A lecher is a fig tree on a cliff: crows get the figs.

113

The road from Sparta to Athens is like the passageway in a house from the men's rooms to the women's.

114

An obol, now, friend, and when the community asks you to contribute for my funeral, you can say you've already given.

115

I was once as young and silly as you are now, but I doubt if you will become as old and wise as I am.

116

Begging from fat Anaximenes, I argued what an advantage it would be to him to share the makings of that paunch with the poor.

117

There is no society without law, no civilization without a city.

118

The only real commonwealth is the whole world.

119

Practice makes perfect.

120

Learn the pleasure of despising pleasure.

121

Education disciplines the young, comforts the old, is the wealth of the poor, and civilizes the rich.

122

The greatest beauty of humankind is frankness.

123

Plato begs too, but like Telemakhos conversing with Athena, with lowered head, so that others may not overhear.

124

Give up philosophy because I'm an old man? It's at the end of a race that you break into a burst of speed.

The Matchmaker

HERONDAS

(The actor sets out his traps while his boy beats a jangling tambourine which, as an audience gathers, gives way to a sprightly jig on a flute. The actor places two stools and opens his box of props and costumes. He dons a dress, a wig, a stole. His eyes are made up female. He trots primly, with swaying hips, to one of the stools, giving a glad eye to the audience on the way. He settles himself, arranges the stole with pompous dignity, bats his eyes, purses his lips, consults an imaginary hand mirror, and becomes an important matron serenely at home. She holds this pose until the boy raps on the box, whereupon her composure is shattered and she yelps on a high note.)

METRIKHÉ

Threissa! Somebody's knocking at the front.
Go see if it's not a country peddler
Selling door to door.

(Actor tosses his stole and wig to the boy, deftly catching a wig of younger, girlish hair, and an apron. He springs to the imaginary door, wiping his hands on the apron, looking dumb and scared. His accent becomes lower class and Thracian. He talks through the closed door.)

THREISSA

Who's there at the door?

(He ventriloquizes the answer.)

GYLLIS

It's me who's here!

THREISSA

Who's me? You're afraid
To come on in, aren't you?

(Horrified by the way she has put the question, covers her mouth with both hands.)

GYLLIS

I'm as in
As I can get till you open the door.

THREISSA

Yes, but who are you?

GYLLIS

It's Gyllis is who.

Philainion's mother. Tell Metrikhé
I've come to pay her sweet self a visit.
(Switches wigs, stole for apron.)

METRIKHÉ

Who is it, pray, at the door?

GYLLIS

It's Gyllis!

Mother Gyllis as ever was!

METRIKHÉ

Gyllis!

(To Threissa, with shooing hands.)
Make yourself scarce, slave. Off with you now, scat.
Gyllis! What stroke of good luck brings you by?
Like a god dropping down on us mortals!
It has been months, five or six, I'll swear,
Since I've had so much as a glimpse of you,
Not even in a dream. And here you are.
(He jumps into the empty space to which she was talking, catching a tackier stole and an old woman's out-of-date bonnet on the way. Stoops at the shoulders, sucks in mouth, draws in on himself, losing height. Voice shaky but chirpy.)

GYLLIS

I don't live near, child, and as for the road
You can sink into the mud past your knees.
I'm as weak as a housefly, anyway.
I'm old, girl. Old age is my shadow now.

METRIKHÉ

Such talk. Exaggeration, all of it.
You wouldn't turn down a nudge, you know it.

GYLLIS

(Cackles.)
Make fun! You young women think we're all
Just like you.

METRIKHÉ

(Pats hair, rolls eyes.)

Well, don't include me, I'm sure!

GYLLIS

What I've come to see you about, my chit,
Is a word to the wise.
(Grins horribly.)
For how long now
Have you been deprived of a husband, dear?
How long alone in your bed? In Egypt,
On a business trip, is he, your Mandris?
It's five months he has been away and not
A letter of the alphabet from him.
(Lets this sink in.)
Hasn't he found another cup to sip?
Hasn't he forgotten you, don't you think?
(Wide-eyed.)
What I've heard of Egypt! Her very home,
The Goddess.
(Pats her groin.)
They've got everything there is,
Everything that grows, everything that's made.
Rich families, gymnasiums, money,
Peace, famous places and philosophers,
Grand sights, army, charming boys, the altar
Of their god who married his own sister.
They have a good king.
(Thinks hard for more.)
A museum. Wine.
Every wonderful thing you might want!
Also, by Koré the bride of Hades,
More women than there are stars in the sky,
And every one of them, dear Metrikhé,
As pretty as the lady goddesses
Who stood naked before Paris that time
To be sized up, forgive the expression.
God forbid they hear me put it like that.
(Averts bad luck with a pious gesture.)
Whatever then can you be thinking of,
My poor girl, to sit here doing nothing?
Bird on an empty nest! All fires go out,

Leaving ashes. Old age is for certain.
Perk up, look about, have a little fun.
Does a ship have only the one anchor?
It has two! When you're dead, you're dead.
Why should this one life be grey and dreary?
(Quietly, reflectively.)
It's uncertain enough for us women.
(Brightens.)
Perhaps you have somebody on the sly?

METRIKHÉ

Of course not!

GYLLIS

Then listen well to me, dear.
I've come here with a jolly little plan.
There is a nice young man, name of Gryllos,
Pataikos' daughter Mataliné's son.
Five prizes in athletics has he won.
One in the Pythian Games at Delphi
When he was a mere stripling of a boy,
Two at Korinthos, the down on his cheeks,
Two at the Olympics, men's boxing match.
(Warms to her subject.)
And he is very well to do, sweetheart.
What's more, he has never mashed the grass down
In that way.
(Proud of her delicacy.)
That is, he is a virgin.
He has yet to press his seal in the wax.
He is still a stranger to Kythera.
(Huddling closer.)
And, Metrikhé, he has fallen for you!
At the festival parade of Misa.
He is turned around, his insides stirred up.
Knowing my skill as a good matchmaker,
He came to me, tears in his handsome eyes,
Pestered me day and night, pitifully,
Near death, and said that love has laid him low.
(Throws her arms wide, and stands hovering.)

Metrikhé, poppet, give Aphrodite
Half a chance, one lovely sweet naughty fling.
We get old, all of us, quite soon enough.
You stand to gain two ways: you'll be loved,
And the boy is both rich and generous.
Look here, think what I am doing for you
And I'm doing it because I love you.

METRIKHÉ

(Sternly, after a longish, shocked silence with downcast eyes.)
You're as blind, Gyllis, as your hair's white.
By Demeter! By my faith in Mandris,
I would not so calmly have abided
Such cheek as this from anybody but you,
And that only because of your years.
I would have given such limping twaddle
Good reason to be lame. Better reason,
Still, to keep away from my door. Make sure,
Old woman, that you don't come here again
With rigmarole not fit for decent ears.
And do let me *sit here doing nothing,*
As you put it. Nobody gets away
With insulting my Mandris to my face.
Not what you came to hear, is it, Gyllis?
(Expels breath in exasperation. Softens manner. Calls over shoulder.)
Threissa! Wipe the black cup clean with a cloth,
Pour a tot in a dribble of water.
Bring Gyllis a little nip for the road.
There, Gyllis, drink up.

GYLLIS

(Hurt.)
Thank you, dear, but no.
(Broods with pouting lip.)
Metrikhé, sweet.
(No reply.)
I'm not here to tempt you.
I'm here on Lady Aphrodite's work.
It was at the festival he found love.
So religious.

METRIKHÉ

(Throws up hands.)

On Aphrodite's work!

GYLLIS

(Primly.)

Yes.

METRIKHÉ

Your health. Drink up. So nice you could come.

GYLLIS

(Philosophically.)

Lovely wine you have, dear. By Demeter.

(Smacks lips.)

Gyllis has never had any better.

(Drains cup, with a lick around the rim.)

I suppose now I'd best be on my way.
Sincerely yours, sweetheart. Keep well, and all.

(Seeming to change the subject.)

Myrtle and Tippy, they keep themselves young.
And myself, I can still shuffle around.

(Actor shuffles, wags his behind, winks broadly, and takes his bow.)

The Whorehouse Manager

HERONDAS

(Battaros, a whorehouse manager, is pleading the case of assault and battery against one Thales, captain of a merchant ship, in a law court in Kos. The actor wears a preposterously big Scythian moustache, a black roachy wig reeking of some fruity essence sharpened by pine oil. His eyes are raccooned with violet circles, his fingers are crowded with trashy rings, his robe is decidedly the color and cut for a dinner party but not for a court of law. He speaks with the brass and vulnerable dignity of an alley lawyer. His accent is foreign, with a trace of a lisp.)

BATTAROS

(In a pitched voice, with gestures.)

Gentlemen of the court, it is not whom
We are, or the prestige we have downtown,
Nor whether Thales here owns a ship which
It is worth one hundred fifty thousand,
Or, as is true, I don't have bread to eat,
But whether he's going to do me dirt
Without he answers to the law for it.

(Gasps, worn out by such eloquence.)

Because if he's to answer to the law,
He's got a sorry lot to answer for,
Which I am about to accuse him of.
A citizen, a man of property,
Is he? Let me tell you, he has a name
Not all that different from mine in town.
We do business as we have to, to live,
Not as we, given a choice, would like to.
He backs the boxer Mennês. Me, I back
The wrestler Aristophon, as is known.
Now this Mennês has won a match or two,
Aristophon can squeeze a breath out yet,
I kid you not. See if you recognize
This Mennês afterdark, but believe me
I will be escorted, rest you assured.

(Waggles eyebrows. Realizes that he has strayed far from what he ought to be saying. Collects thoughts, takes aim, and gets back to his subject.)

Thales' plea, no doubt, is going to be
He brought a cargo of wheat from Akês
Back when we had the famine. Fine and good!
I import girls from Tyros. How is this
With the people? He did not bring them wheat
And *give* it to them. Nor are my girls free.
He seems to think they are though, free gratis.
If he means, because he crosses the sea,
Because he wears a coat costs three hundred
In Attika, if he means, while I wear
This thin old shirt and these worn-out sandals
And keep house on the dry land, if he means
He can get away with forcing a girl
Behind my back, in the middle of the night,
Me sound asleep for hours in my bed,
To run away with him, then I submit
This city's no longer safe to live in.
No, not safe to live in, our proud city!
Where then is all our boasting and boosting?
He undermines us, this Thales, who should,
Like me, know his place, keep to his level,
Like me, respectful to all citizens.
(Shakes his head sadly.)
Such is not the case. The real uppercrust,
People with a name, they obey the laws.
They don't get me out of bed at midnight,
They don't beat me up, set fire to my house,
Haul off one of my girls against her will.
But this wildman Phrygian calling himself
Thales, whose name, gentlemen, used to be
Artimmês, has done all of the above,
Scoffing the law and the magistracy.
Now if you please, Clerk of Court, read us all
The law on assault. Let's have the timer
Plug the water clock while he reads it out,
Or
(Making a joke, very sure of himself.)

it'll look, as the man said, as if
He's put his bladder down for a carpet.

CLERK OF COURT

(Actor has only to stand straight, assume a voice of wheezy public rectitude, and read from an imaginary scroll.)

Whensoever any freeman shall do . . .

BATTAROS

(Taking over, from memory. He has done his homework.)

. . . a mischief unto a female slave or
Belabor her with improper intent,
His fine therefor shall be double the fine
For assault. These, gentlemen, are the words
Of Khairondas in the Code, not the words
Of one Battaros, plaintiff, bringing suit
Against one Thales, so called, defendant.
Likewise, if any man beat down a door
His fine must be no less than a mina.
And if any man set fire to a house
Or break into and enter same, his fine
Shall be one thousand drakhmas, damages
Twice that. Khairondas in the code lays down
The laws for running a city, but you,
Thales, what do you care for any law?
One day you're off in Brikindera,
Another, in Abdera. Tomorrow,
If you could get passage, you would be off
To Phaselis. And I, to speak bluntly
And to not wear out your ears, gentlemen,
And get to the point, I have been done by
Thales like the mouse in the tar bucket.
I have been hit by his fist. My front door,
Which put me back four obols to have set,
Charged to my rent the month I had it up,
Is split, and my lintel is scorched and charred.
And — come here, Myrtalê, come testify —

(Actor leads forward an imaginary girl.)

Let the court see you. Don't be bashful now.
All these people, look, are trying your case.

Think of them as your fathers and brothers.
(Indignantly, to the court.)
Would you look, gentlemen, at her torn dress.
(Lifts her dress.)
Look her all over, see how she is bruised
And manhandled by this ape of a man.
He has pulled every hair out of her thing!
Plucked her clean as a chicken! Were I young —
He can be thankful for my age — he would
Have breathed his own blood, I can promise you,
(Dramatic pause.)
Like Philippos the Locust of Samos.
(Pause, to follow this classical allusion with meaningful silence, which does not achieve the effect intended.)
You can laugh?
(With a furious and futile look, soon abandoned for desperate honesty.)
So I am a pederast.
I admit it. My name is Battaros.
Sisymbras my grandfather before me
And Sisymbriskos my father were both,
As I am, in the whorehouse business.
(Ranting.)
If I were stronger, I'd choke a lion
If, by Zeus, the lion's name was Thales!
(Recovers himself, rearranges his thoughts. Turns to Thales, pointing at him.)
Like as not, let's say, you love Myrtalê,
Nothing at all peculiar about that.
Me, I love a square meal. I get the one,
You get the other. That's only business.
You're feeling horny, that's natural.
What you do is pay Battaros the price
And you can bash what you've bought as you will.
(Turns to the judges.)
One point more, gentlemen, and this for you,
Not him. There were, you know, no witnesses.
You must judge this case on the face of it.
If all Thales wanted was to beat up

A poor slave and wants her to testify
Under torture, then I will take her place.
Willingly! But he must pay just the same
If he hurts me, just as if I were her.
Did Minos balance this case on his scales,
Could he try it a better way than this?
To sum up, gentlemen: if you decide
For me, it will not be for Battaros
But for all businessmen not citizens.
(Finger in air, orating.)
Now's the time to show the mettle of Kos,
Of great Merops and his proud daughter Kos!
Glory of Thessalos and Herakles!
The place Asklepios came from Trikka!
The Place where Phoibé gave birth to Leto!
Ponder all this, bring in a right judgment,
And unless all that we've heard about Phrygians
Is wrong, he will be improved by the lash.
(Bows low, with sweep of the hand, and a smirk.)

[The Little Boy] Mime XIII

HERONDAS

Playing blind man's bluff, banging a cookpot,
Flying a junebug tethered by a thread,
Destroying Granpa's afternoon nap.
(*The rest is lost*.)